AN ARCTIC ADVENTURE

An Arctic Adventure

ROY S. PETERS

The Pentland Press
Edinburgh – Cambridge – Durham – USA

First published in 1997 by
The Pentland Press Ltd
1 Hutton Close,
South Church
Bishop Auckland
Durham

ISBN 1-85821-514-5

Typeset by Carnegie Publishing, 18 Maynard St, Preston
Printed and bound by Antony Rowe Ltd, Chippenham

To my Aunt May who encouraged my writing from an early age but who died before she had a chance to read the desk-top published manuscript.

Contents

Chapter I

Initial Thoughts

I suppose that our story starts in the autumn of 1992 with the arrival on the doormat of a brochure for 'the World's Most Beautiful Voyage'. I say 'suppose' because that arrival could have been initiated by either one of two possibilities for which I was responsible. Thus, it could either have been by my sending off a coupon from *Radio Times*, or a card from an unsolicited pile for holidays and insurance. Whatever the reason, I welcomed this brochure which was totally different from normal central European productions by the major touring and holiday firms. For one thing, an eleven-day tour really lasts twelve days rather than ten days! For another, it wasn't a cruise or a holiday in the usual sense. It was for a voyage on a 'working boat' that carries cargo and random passengers, being both a heavy lorry and a bus on a waterbound route. It goes at fifteen knots up the Norwegian coast and back again for a total round trip of 2,500 miles.

Like many other brochures that gave my mind options for holidays, it was filed away, untidily, should it ever become needed, because at that time, in 1992, the price seemed more than the average – but it *did* show beautiful scenery in the Norwegian Fjords that I'd learned about long ago. So it was filed but not forgotten. It would be a 'voyage of exploration' rather than a holiday!

In the autumn of 1993, on contemplating possibilities for

using up my 'leave' from the Civil Service, my mind ranged through the European brochures again – and hit on a Nile Cruise listed therein (not a European Nile, but the real African one!). I had travelled by that company before and obtained less than complete satisfaction, but more than that, inoculations and injections (Yugh!) were required for the journey. That was presumably, I thought, because of the higher temperatures that cause insects and bugs (the little buggers!) to thrive. Maybe one had better try for something cooler (like the Norwegian tour) and so the idea had been resurrected. That, to me, was a contrast worth considering. There, surely, in the Arctic Circle, one would not have to worry with either heat or the bugs!

Chapter II

Decisions and Planning

The decision of whether to go to the popular play areas of Europe, still unreasonably warm, or whether to try the as-yet-unvisited stunning coast of Norway was easy – as I am far happier in cool climates than in the overpowering sun and temperatures of 70 degrees or more. So I recontacted the Norwegian State Railway Office in London concerning the possibility of obtaining an up-to-date fare and schedules booklet. One of my initial concerns was the language problem because I know none of the language apart from that which appears on Norwegian postage stamps. The London NSR office assured me that there is no problem because ' . . . all Norwegians speak English!'

The fares had increased by about 10 per cent but the same types of boats and cabins were still available. They offered a summer as well as a winter service. In fact, as I already knew, at 10 p.m., every night of the year, a boat leaves Bergen going north by a very meandering route to Kirkenes and back – taking eleven days. Kirkenes, in the extreme north-east of Norway, is only three miles from the Russian border. The brochures for that winter (1993/94) hadn't been reissued yet but the girl promised to send me a new 'Winter Schedule' which would be useful for planning purposes. This I welcomed, not so much for the important times but more for the types of cabin on each boat.

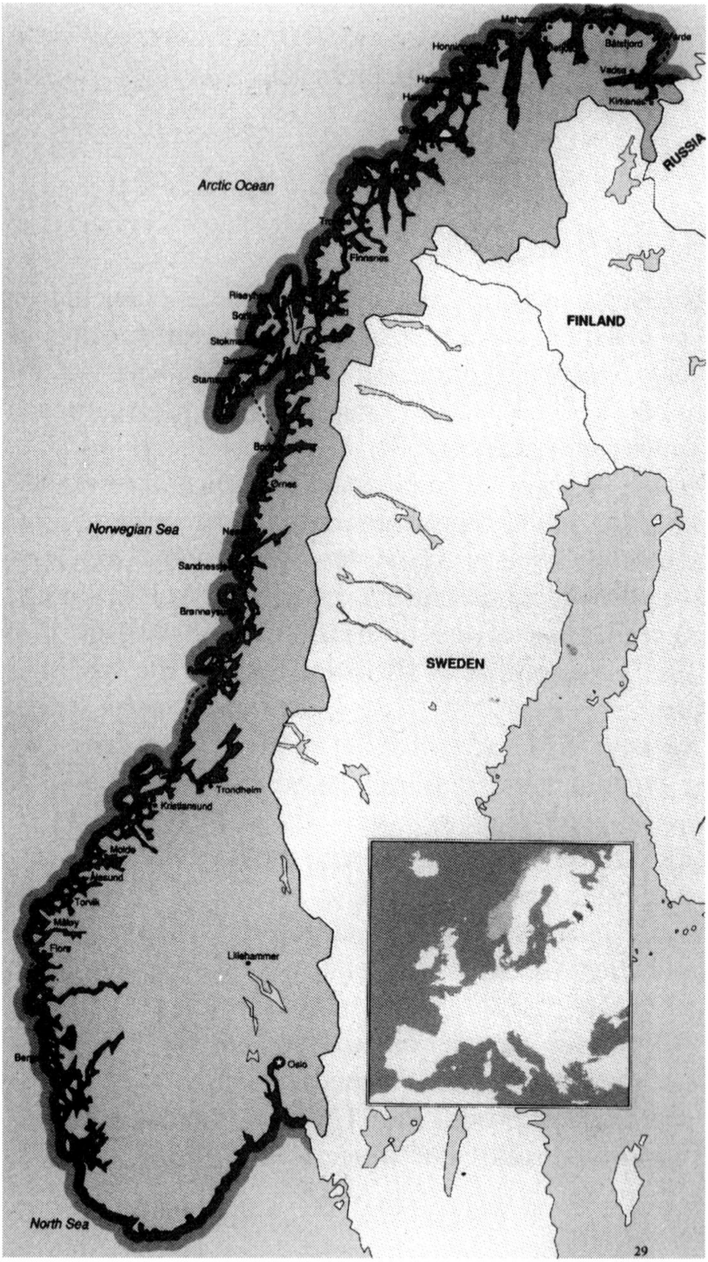
Båtsfjord
Vadsø
Kirkenes
RUSSIA
Arctic Ocean
Finnsnes
FINLAND
Ørnes
Norwegian Sea
SWEDEN
Trondheim
Kristiansund
Molde
Ålesund
Torvik
Måløy
Florø
Lillehammer
Oslo
North Sea
29

The boats, some modern, some traditional, were owned and operated by five companies in Norway, giving a combined fleet of eleven boats, all integrated into one service.

The schedule, or 'Sailings Listing', duly arrived and I studied the boats, their types, their cabins and the dates in a careful process of selection and elimination. Firstly, I chose to go for one of the *traditional* boats with character, rather than a floating version of the Ritz. This eliminated less than half because the majority are traditional! Then came the choice of cabin. The aim was for economy because the mileage is high and so are Norwegian prices. So my eyes and mind 'homed in' on a *single* cabin with basic facilities. After all, the idea is to look at scenery and the Aurora Borealis, so the cabin is not really even a secondary consideration. I was going to buy a return ticket from Malvern to the North Pole (effectively) – complete with three meals a day at sea. I hoped it wouldn't be too choppy!

The D1 cabin-type was my selected first choice, being better than E, not as plush as C, and for one person. Just having a washbasin would be adequate for a male with long legs – but were mine long enough? [An extra £300, approximately, would be required for the additional luxury of shower and WC!] So that gives an indication of their coded notation! As luck would have it, only the traditional boats had my required sort of cabin, so I was able to choose from the following vessels:

Finnmarken (148 berths)
Harald Jarl (165)
Kong Olav (224)
Lofoten (228)
Nord Norge (207)
Nordstjernon (180)

Polarlys (170)
Ragnald Jarl (142)

I still had quite a choice – so the next factors to consider were the date and route options. The brochure showed that NSR (the Norwegian State Railways) would either fly or sail passengers to the start point in Bergen. Sailings from the UK would normally be from Newcastle upon Tyne, whereas flights would be on their selected aircraft from Heathrow. These transfers would be included in their overall (slightly different) fares. An interesting feature of the flight option was that passengers would be given free accommodation in a good medium hotel in Bergen for an extra night after the completion of the eleven days on the boat. Flying from Heathrow, rather than sailing from Newcastle, was, on the whole, more economical in time and costs, and allowed an extra day's free sightseeing in Bergen. I could now schedule a list of possible departure dates from Malvern and know where I would be each day of each option.

The next criterion was *not* to use British Rail on Sundays, either way, as the Malvern-Paddington service runs only in the afternoon. That cut out more options and left possible start dates from Malvern as 3, 5, 9, 11 or 12 November.

The next criterion was to choose who I wanted to *miss least* at the **End of the Trail Country Music Club** at Ombersley in Worcestershire. As I had already seen one of the duos several times before, I chose to go for the earlier pair of dates (3rd and 5th) to allow me to see an act, another duo, that I'd never seen before. That meant a choice of either the *Lofoten* (with its 228 berths and built in 1964) or the *Ragnald Jarl* (142 berths and built in 1956). Well, I thought, maybe the *Lofoten* has eight years less rust on it, so that'll be my first choice, giving a 'departure' from

Bergen of 4 November. The fare would be £994 (including the Heathrow to Bergen return flights) plus £16 rail fare (reduced from the standard price because of NSR) plus £18 insurance – provided that they had a berth available!

The London office of NSR was not yet networked to the computers in Norway so they would have to contact their Norwegian colleagues by phone. Because of the closure of that office on Saturdays, they were expecting a response on the Monday, 20 September 1993. They later confirmed the provisional booking and gave me a reference number to quote on the formal booking form.

That booking form was sent off on 21 September 1993 and the formal booking acknowledged on 27 September, although my full documentation was to arrive later. The full complement of papers – travel tickets for 'trains and boats and planes' – arrived on 8 October 1993. I then acquired some Norwegian kroner (about 10 to the £) and a quantity of traveller's cheques – all via my friendly building society in Great Malvern. So it was now 'all systems go' for my adventure to the Frozen North. I produced a schedule of my movements for friends, relations and colleagues, and this is shown in Annex A. Maybe I had better buy some really appropriate clothing!

A review of suitable clothing showed that I was reasonably well equipped already. As indicated earlier, the cold doesn't bother me; I prefer it to the heat. Even on ordinary cold days, for which I bought my *parka* several years ago, I am happy in ordinary jackets and shirts. When I first reported on my parka's suitability for the UK winters (I had 'cooked' inside it) I remarked, long ago, that it 'would be more appropriate to the North Pole's weather than here! If ever I go to the North Pole it might be worth taking!'

Naturally the parka was on my list to pack. However, until such time as I got far enough north 'not to cook' in it, I would use a lined jacket, also obtained years ago through my friend Bill Taylor on one of his trips to Ledbury market in Herefordshire. I seem to remember it costing £3.50 then. The lined jacket in its turn would also 'cook' me if I wore it too early, but it would do for intermediate temperatures between the 'polar regions' and south-western Norway. For the first few hundred miles, or so, I would wear an ordinary jacket, too thick for use in the UK except in winters, which I had acquired a few years before from 'Change Gear', a useful shop that used to exist in Malvern Link. Headgear is included with the parka, having its own hood, but I would take my 'Russian-type' hat, bought in Magg's of Malvern about ten years previously, for use with the ordinary and lined jackets.

The only new purchases required were better gloves and a few pairs of thermal socks for the Arctic itself. I already had acceptable, treaded walking boots in case the 'going' became slippery. I had used these boots in the UK for hill and fell walking, although only occasionally as they are difficult and long-winded to put on. In the Arctic, with its longer hours of darkness, there would be more time for such activities, and so the Malvern market provided my only new needs (gloves and thermal socks) in late October before the 'off'.

Chapter III

Getting to the Start

On the day of the 'off', I was wished 'Bon Voyage' by Annie Courtenage, who founded and runs Annie's Country & Western Club in Malvern – and Brenda, who runs her own very useful and friendly 'Alterations' shop near home. The latter provides what I deem a very useful facility for a bachelor with deteriorating eyesight. The taxi-cab from DG Cabs arrived at the appointed time and sped me to the Malvern Link Station, with much bemusement for the driver that I had got a return ticket from Malvern Link to the North Pole! There, a cloudy sky lay low over the 'Waiting Room', as BR calls its portacabin on the up-line platform at Malvern Link Station.

The InterCity Express sped me even more quickly and smoothly on my way to Paddington British Rail station in London. Calm, almost still, waters ran below the Severn Bridge at Worcester, with distant mists giving a typical November feel to the scene. British Rail's 'standard' compartments were remarkably comfortable and clean, somehow eerie with their high-tech automatic doors, which appeared to have minds of their own – unless that was in eagerness to anticipate each passenger's move. The ticket inspector incorrectly punched my ticket and apologized, no doubt because of the non-standard format of the NSR ticket, which on the subsequent return trip was deemed in order.

The case-humping phase was now about to begin as I

lugged the overpacked cases from Paddington Station to the Tregaron Hotel in Norfolk Square. My hands and heart survived but, after checking in, I found myself on the long haul up to the third floor, to a room that I had often used whilst on official business. Recovery time was remarkably quick, as I settled into the room which was actually in the Ashley Hotel. Several years ago, the management had acquired three adjoining hotels, the Tregaron, Ashley and Oasis!

As usual in the UK, the room was over-heated and I was obliged to turn the heating off in order to survive. I then had a comfortable, leisurely evening in that room – the usual Room No. 8 – consuming a selection of sandwiches that I had packed in Malvern. Later on I visited a new (for me) restaurant called the 'Chef's Hat' in Praed Street rather than my more normal 'Mickey's Fish Bar' which I had used for decades.

Back in the hotel, I mixed pleasures between the TV, the radio and the self-help coffee facilities. Being of a musical disposition, I enjoyed the Radio 2 offerings of folk dancing complete with a 'caller' on Radio (you've got to believe it!), a feature on Ewan McColl, his music and songs and a Nana Mouskouri programme.

Having retired to bed at 9.30 p.m. to build up reserves of energy for the coming fortnight, I was prevented from rest and relaxation by some noisy young men and old boys with their fireworks. Being already 3 November, I suppose it was understandable – but most nights in Norfolk Square present the weary traveller and workaholic with inconsiderate noisy people. These firework explosions ricochetted around the canyons of the Paddington area with a similar effect that they would have had in a closed-cave system.

Worse than that, some peoples' car alarms were set off by the fireworks, wailing well into the night. These alarms then triggered other alarms in a chain reaction until the 'canyons' were alive with the sound, not of music, but of dozens of car alarms. It was at that point that I thought, 'If the rest of the fortnight is as eventful as this, I had better take notes for a possible short story that I could write.' The structure of the book already began to evolve.

Eventually, I dozed off, until a noisy morning arrived. Dark as well! Putting the light on to check the time, I saw that it was still only 12.20 a.m. Rowdy voices in adjacent rooms were another inconsiderate distraction. However, everywhere quietened down by about 2 a.m. and my long-awaited sleep began after 4 a.m.! I reawoke at 6 a.m. Being the day that my expedition started, it seemed not too inappropriate to get up for a brief trip to the toilet before returning for my *real* relaxation until 6.50 a.m.

Much more excited now, I humped my case from my room on the 3rd floor, down the narrow stairs to the 2nd floor and thence via a wider stairway to the ground floor. Nice to get that job out of the way before breakfast!

The hotel served a normal English breakfast – quite appropriate for a Welsh management and Thai girl waitresses! I polished off some bread and jam for some sustenance to enable me to keep going until my 'New World'.

Leaving the hotel at 7.50 a.m., I lugged the case and my cabin baggage to the Circle Line station at Paddington. Only a few stops were necessary on this line before changing at Gloucester Road to the Piccadilly Line for Heathrow. That's where the first problem was! A tannoy announcement explained the fact that there was a security alert at King's Cross, that there would be obvious delays and some reroutings would be necessary. Furthermore, there were signal problems on the District Line and personal reroutings were also recommended there.

However, I arrived safe and sound, and in time, at the 'Heathrow 1, 2, 3' station which I needed for Terminal 3. The next things to sort out were the multiple entrances to the Terminal Building – I wanted Scandinavian Airlines – yes, it was the SAS that was taking me! It was easy to find, but a very long walk – especially with all that luggage! Having got in, I found an empty check-in desk and checked in at 9.20 a.m. The case weighed a legal 16 kilos and I received my boarding pass, showing my passport for the first of many times. The desk also wanted a few simple questions answered.

I waited in the main Departure Lounge and watched all the displays. My flight (SK 516) didn't yet have a 'gate' assigned to it, so I made use of the pre-flight toilets. On studying the boarding pass whilst waiting, I saw that I had indeed got a seat in a non-smoking area – specifically, number 22C, a gangway seat. I took my second Stugeron at 9.48 a.m. to counter any motion-sickness tendencies and awaited further developments with interest.

An announcement stated that any unattended luggage would be removed and *destroyed*, which seemed a sensible warning – so I kept a close eye on mine! At 9.58 a.m. the flight information board displayed:

SK 516 1040 GATE OPEN 53

which indicated the start of another walk, this time to Gate 53. It was a long trek of progressively tighter filtering

through the required gates until '53' was reached eventually at 10.14 a.m. There were no extending *fingers* to plug flight SK 516 in to the building to ease our passage. What they cunningly arranged, purely for our exercise, was for us to walk downstairs to catch a bus which would take us to the plane. That's progress?

At 10.24 a.m., about three dozen of us boarded the bus which moved off at 10.31 a.m. and took us to the patiently waiting aircraft, named 'Rollo Viking'. It was a type which I hadn't seen before but which reminded me of a BAC111 or a Caravelle. No external markings gave any clues! I got seated in a surprisingly comfortable position devoid of tobacco smoke, ready to enjoy my trip, which was not direct to Bergen but via Stavanger. The announcement confirmed this, saying that Stavanger was one and a half hours away.

The mystery aircraft, belonging to the SAS (Scandinavian Airlines – not what you're thinking!), lumbered down the runway and, after thirty-two seconds, it 'rotated' at 11.05 a.m. for the take-off to Norway. It climbed steeply until it got above the clouds, giving the first sight of the sun that I'd had in days. Once at a steady altitude, lunch was served – this being a very attractive salad based on salmon and chicken. The sweet course turned out to be nutty chocolate mousse. Delicious! I was given a copy of the *Independent* newspaper to pass away the time above the clouds. A crew member identified the aircraft as an MD82 (i.e. it is made by McDonnell Douglas).

I saw my first Norwegian islands at 13.13 hrs on our approach to Stavanger (Norway adheres uniformly to the 24-hour clock, lucky to say!). We had naturally changed from GMT by adding an hour during the flight. The initial surprise with this scene was that it wasn't snowy at all, but was a green and pleasant land, the large number of waterways and islands making it a stunning panorama. Touchdown was at 13.34 hrs, very shortly followed by a great surge of reverse thrust to decelerate before the very long taxying phase to the Terminal.

After a brief interchange of passengers at the airport, the aircraft moved out to the runway, accelerated for twenty-eight seconds and then took-off at 14.04 hrs. The short leg to Bergen carried us over many beautiful islands and we reached there in the pouring rain. Nevertheless, great oodles of reverse thrust slowed us down and prepared us for taxying.

Because of the increases in walk-lengths at airports nowadays, I decided, this time, to get a trolley for my luggage. They certainly handle better than the average UK supermarket trolley! The next thing was to find the bus to transport us to Bergen as planned, but several walks around the exterior of the terminal revealed no bus with the NSR marking. I went back inside and found myself next to a genial guy with a **PETERS** card, which he emphasized and held close to his chest. My face lit up and I gave him a 'thumbs-up' sign to indicate that we were the people looking for each other. He led me to his minibus in which I was the only passenger from the airport to the Quay from which the boat would depart. The minibus set off a little later than the scheduled 14.45 hrs, but the journey was a beautiful one with a rocky-inlet landscape, fjords and mountains along its twelve-mile route. The first Norwegian that I was to have conversation with in his own country certainly spoke English – a good start Roy!

Chapter IV

The Highway to the Arctic Circle

I left the minibus and went to my Arctic chariot, declining the offer of a shopping trip to Vestre from which I'd be returned later – all at no extra cost. I had known about this in advance, but opted for unpacking and settling into my cabin, and hopefully receiving further documentation, including a booklet specific to this trip.

I had arrived at the *Lofoten* at the Frielenesquay at about 15.15 hrs fully in the knowledge that the departure was not until 22.00 hrs and that the 24-hour cafeteria didn't open until 19.00 hrs. Thereafter, it would be *continuously* open. The deciding factor to opt out of the shopping visit was because of the piss-istent rain. Far better to get used to my room and its environs which I would explore.

I found the 'Reception' (spelt 'Resepsjon') just up a ramp into the boat; the receptionist said that my cabin was ready and he led me to it. (How did he remember me with all the numbers involved? It meant that now we had at least two Norwegians who spoke English!) I got the cabin to feel like home which, indeed, it would be for the next eleven days – and then explored the vessel whilst it was still in the harbour. I looked at the scene from the shelter of the boat mainly, as the rain was a deterrent to walking outside.

As darkness fell on the harbour and its surrounds, the lights created a beautifully romantic air that wasn't apparent in daylight. This was despite, or maybe because of, the

FFR

P.O.Box 308
N-9601 Hammerfest

Tel. +47 84 11000
Fax: +47 8412773

M/S «LOFOTEN»

TELEPHONE ONBOARD: 090-92299. TELEFAX ONBOARD: 090-98075

Type of cabin/category	Total cabins	Total berths
Outs. doubles sh/t, sep. bedr. cat. L2	1	2
Outs. doubles sh/t .... cat. S2	4	8
Outs. doubles sh/t .... cat. A2	28	56
Outs./ins. doubles sh/t......... cat. B2	7	14
Outs./ins. singles .... cat. D1	10	10
Outs./ins. doubles................ cat. D2	9	18
Outs./ins. singles .... cat. D3	3	9
Outs./ins. doubles................ cat. E2	22	44
Outs./ins. 4-beds .... cat. E4	12	48
TOTAL..	96	209
Hospital: Ins. 3-berths sh/t.................. cat. B3	1	3

CAR SPACE	6 CARS
MAX. WEIGHT	1,5 TONS
MAX. HEIGHT	1.90 M.

BR. T.	2597 TONS
LENGTH O.A	87.4 M.
BEAM	13.2 M.
DRAUGHT	4.6 M.
SPEED	16 KNOTS
BUILT	1964
REBUILT	1985
DECKS	5 + BRIDGE

ELECTRICAL EQUIPMENT 220 V.A.C.

Finnmark Fylkesrederi og Ruteselskap
Marketing departement
Booking and information:
Telephone: +47 84 14344. Telefax: +47 84 14655. Telex: 64257
(From 28.10.93: Tel.: +47 78 41 10 00/78 41 43 44. Fax.: +47 78 41 46 55)

Hurtigruten - Norges riksvei nr. 1

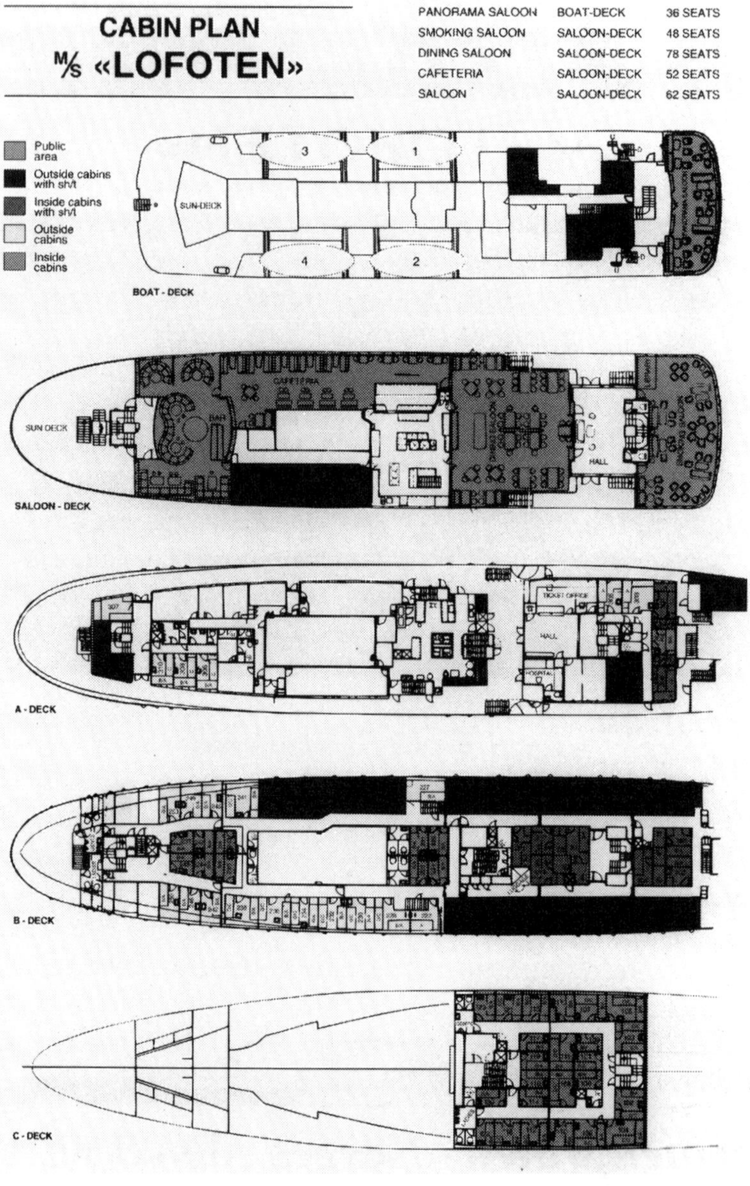
CABIN PLAN
M/S «LOFOTEN»
PANORAMA SALOON BOAT-DECK 36 SEATS
SMOKING SALOON SALOON-DECK 48 SEATS
DINING SALOON SALOON-DECK 78 SEATS
CAFETERIA SALOON-DECK 52 SEATS
SALOON SALOON-DECK 62 SEATS
Public area
Outside cabins with sh/t
Inside cabins with sh/t
Outside cabins
Inside cabins
SUN-DECK
BOAT - DECK
SUN DECK
CAFETERIA
HALL
SALOON - DECK
TICKET OFFICE
HALL
HOSPITAL
A - DECK
B - DECK
C - DECK

combination of rain and the lights. It was just *interesting* by day, but t'was more beautiful at night with the natural darkness and rain being lit by a myriad of lights around the harbour. Pity that there wasn't anyone present to share these feelings with. However, as the eleven days and nights went by, being alone with my own thoughts, activities and experiences would be a *bonus!* I would see things that I had learned about many years ago at school. Solitude would help me to recount my thoughts and impressions of the trip. I surveyed the harbour from all aspects and levels of the vessel.

The lady in the cafeteria whom I approached for refreshments at 19.20 hrs said, 'Are you Mr Peters?' (Never seen her in my life before – honestly!) I answered in the affirmative. She told me that despite the lack of a meal, which was normal on the first night, could I please join the Captain on this occasion in the restaurant? Again, I gave an affirmative response and she showed me to my 'special table' in a corner near the windows. It would be my 'reserved table' for the whole trip. She would ask an English-speaking Norwegian if he might like to share it with me, as I was the only English person on board. So I had a meal – rather than refreshments – consisting of Norwegian soup and a buffet of cheeses and meats. The Captain introduced himself, wished me happiness on the trip, and gave me some 'reading matter' which was in a package and included a brochure of the voyage. I already knew that this route had, for years, been known as Highway 1. Moreover, *Hurtigrute* means Express Route.

At 22.00 hrs, the vessel slowly got under way, passing the magic fairy lights in the harbour, into the fjord, witnessed something that might have been an oil rig, but was too dark to discern, and settlements at the water's edge. As we moved out further from Bergen along a sparsely lit network of fjords, I was entertained by a self-appointed male voice choir in straw hats, boaters etc. They were singing and drinking everywhere on the boat. They were mostly youngsters – like college boys – singing numbers like 'Raindrops keep falling on my head' and many others. The music was unmistakable but the words were Norwegian, creating quite an atmosphere.

I turned in to my cabin after indulging in this atmosphere, going to bed very happy. Around 01.00 hrs I was awoken by the gentle rolling of our craft. By 01.15 hrs, the severity of this rolling had increased causing my bedside drink in its Tupperware beaker (only water, your Honour!) to tip off the chair which was acting as my bedside table! It was 5 November 1993.

By 02.15 hrs the roll amplitudes had increased after a period of comparative calm. What an introduction to coastal waters! I got washed and dressed by 03.45 hrs and went to the 24-hour cafeteria for some coffee and cake at 04.00. I could see many reasons for and advantages of the 24-hour service. I also established that my legs weren't long enough, really, for the D1 cabin's relatively primitive facilities. My thick, hard-backed copy of *Jurassic Park* would have come in handy during this trip!

At Florø, I watched the loading and unloading of cargo by the skilful crane operator aboard our vessel. A couple got off but no new passengers got on. I, and the singers, wandered off onto the quay, exchanged pleasantries and returned to the boat for its journey northwards. I stayed awake through the narrowing fjords to Maløy – all in virtually total darkness – a pleasant experience as the diesel-powered craft crept its way through the narrow waterways.

At Maløy, after watching the start of the operations, I perhaps understandably fell asleep, as I hadn't had much rest during that exciting night thus far.

The reader may wonder why anyone should want to go to the Arctic Circle, particularly in winter. What is so special about the Arctic Circle and places north of it? In order not to digress at this stage, the reasons why I consider the Arctic to be so special are shown in Annex B. It is not that one falls off the edge of the world there, but the world *does* have different properties from the non-Arctic regions. It is the area of the globe north of 66°33′ N (that angle is 90° less the Earth's tilt to its orbit).

Later that same morning, I woke up and proceeded to the restaurant as the vessel continued to roll excessively. I *could* eat breakfast under these conditions (surprise! surprise!), and furthermore, I enjoyed the amazing view from my breakfast windows whilst having a 'Norwegian' (similar to 'Continental') breakfast. We had very cloudy but attractive conditions. The camera indicated that 'it is too dark for any photos, unless under flash within seven feet of the camera' so I couldn't record the views. This was *late* morning too! Later, I risked it anyway with the Herøy Bridge to Torvik taken through the window of the large observation lounge at the front of the vessel. Had the flash not gone off (no option with this particular automatic) it would have been a reasonable low-light photo without the reflected flash from the window. Half an hour before this, I had seen my first snowy mountain of the trip. Also, I had evidence of cleaning operations on board as a cleaning lady did my cabin whilst docked at Torvik.

Before the midday arrival at Alesund, I studied the information on the town in the brochure which the Captain had left me. The two main items of interest to me would be the aquarium and Aksla mountain (a hill, really). I planned, in my mind, the walk around the harbour to head for the aquarium first, noting the point where I could turn off for an ascent of Aksla mountain. I took the brochure map with me as a constant guide for paths and roads, and headed round the harbour towards the aquarium. A woman from the boat seemed to be taking a long route to the town even though she had seen me studying the map on the boat. I wondered if I ought to offer helpful suggestions. However, her constant stopping for window-shopping would have put my sightseeing schedule in jeopardy, had I gone back, so I continued to the aquarium having passed the Aksla mountain turnoff point. On my arrival at the aquarium (no obvious entry sign) which was in a backstreet, I found no one around, so gingerly investigated the interior of the building. I managed to find my way in but no one occupied the reception/ticket desk for what was obviously the aquarium. Having waited in vain for a while for someone to appear, I progressed further inside and came across a small but very interesting collection of fish. Some I had *never* seen before in *any* aquarium, large or small. In virtual solitude, I viewed all the exhibits and went out the way that I had come in, which actually seemed to be the exit anyway – there appeared to be no entrance! Still, zero cost for a small show wasn't bad. Carry on Roy!

Retracing the route to the turnoff for Aksla mountain, and looking at the map and my watch, I deemed there to be sufficient time remaining before the boat's departure to make an 'ascent'. Through the network of hilly streets bordering on the fjord, I climbed to the local park that led to the foot of the hill, hardly a mountain. My map showed the paths clearly, so I ascended by one route and descended by another, which is my normal practice if maps are good enough. The view from the top revealed a bird's-eye panorama of the town, which is built on three islands. After descending to the middle of the park, I saw the familiar face of the apparently lost lady who I had left to her window-shopping earlier. Her command of English was poor, but infinitely better than my knowledge of Norwegian, and so we chatted on the way back to the boat. She had apparently learned English at school but had forgotten much of it, although fortunately not all. I learned that she wasn't going far on the Hurtigrute – indeed, this was where she changed to go home to the island of Runde. Readers of this may well remember Runde featuring on UK nature programmes on television. It is famous for its bird inhabitants, notably for its delightful puffins, which are a protected species. Runde is, in fact, Norway's largest bird-rock, and also has thirty-one other species amongst its half a million nesting birds (who counted them, I wonder?). We parted company at the point where she turned off to catch her 'bus' home. 'Bus' is the English word that she used, but it may well be a loose translation of whatever it was in Norwegian, bearing in mind the fact that boats are used for everything in this beautiful country.

The boat sailed at 15.00 hrs, returning to its northward trek. After a late midday meal, I watched through the front lounge windows as we approached Molde and the Romsdal Alps. The view of these Alps from Molde is, undoubtedly, one of the scenic highlights on this trip when viewed by daylight. There are eighty-seven snow-capped peaks to be seen in one gorgeous panorama. The philosophy of the trip, according to the brochure, was to call, in at least one direction, on all places in the daytime. So our 18.00 hrs departure from Molde might be offset by a different departure time a few days later when travelling south. Checking the schedule I saw that a different time had indeed been allocated, namely 21.15 hrs! Molde on the northbound route was considered the *daytime* stop. Of course, at any other time than winter it would be light. Disappointments are bound to happen. I then surveyed the schedule to see whether I would miss anything else major in both directions. I noticed one further disappointment would occur further north, namely the spectacular Lofoten mountains would be in darkness in both directions. That is *the* disadvantage of having just a couple of hours daylight per day. It might be advisable to consider the phases of the moon, which I had not included in my planning, when visiting Norway in the winter. I would remember next time. The very thin crescent moon during this trip didn't provide enough light for even the human eye, let alone my camera!

By this time, I was very weary and not in a frame of mind for sightseeing, entirely due, I believed, to the lack of sleep the previous night, plus my wanting to see everything, both day and night. Because of this 'not with it' feeling, I decided there and then to get some proper overnight sleep as it was dark anyway, and make absolutely full use of the available daylight later. That meant sightseeing, from the several decks of our vessel, along the unique coastal scenery, and using every moment available for exploring ashore from the moment of docking to casting off.

But the night *had* to be reserved for sleep so that I was fit to enjoy the restricted hours of daylight to the full. Maybe the night was meant for sleep, but I would have real reasons for sightseeing at night – the Aurora Borealis was one of my reasons for being there!

Anyhow, no Aurora tonight, or the previous night for that matter, due to the overcast and very cloudy conditions. Thus *sleep* was the number one priority that night, especially as we had our longest stop ashore the next day when there would be six hours in Trondheim, from 06.00 hrs until 12.00 noon.

But it wasn't such a good night after all! The open-sea stretch from the exit of the Molde Fjord near Bud as far as Kristiansund provided an excellent opportunity for the *Lofoten* to practice its rock 'n' roll gyrations! After the arrival at Kristiansund, following that wildish journey, I just lay on my cabin bed whilst we were at the quay from 21.00 to 23.00 hrs. Peeping at the scene through the venetian blinds was quite sufficient! I did however leave my bunk to visit the 24-hour cafeteria for more coffee and cake. Then a return to bed seemed a sensible move. Tomorrow would be 6 November.

I awoke and looked through the blinds at 06.10 hrs. We'd arrived in Trondheim. I got up and walked on the cold quayside, perused a town map, and went back to my cabin to write cards to friends and relations before my Norwegian breakfast. I then ventured further afield having compared the map at the quayside with that in my book from the Malvern library. From that information, and having looked at the Captain's brochures, I decided to visit Nidaros Cathedral, known to the locals as the Domkirken, and also the old fort, known as the Kristiansten Festning. This was situated at the top of a hill with, it was said, lovely views of the city and its surrounds.

I would first go to Nidaros Cathedral by way of the

Kjøpmannsgata and turn left into its own precinct just before Bispegata. This took me to the rear entrance, but I walked clockwise around the medieval building, which looked like any other grey building, only revealing its really decorative part at the front. There were very many statues built into the vast facade, some clothed, some unclothed, with one even of St Denis which I remembered from Notre Dame in Paris, easily recognisable because he carried his head on a plate.

It was difficult to take photos in the very low light. However I attempted one full-frontal of Nidaros Cathedral after I'd taken a frontal close-up. The negatives turned out, as expected, somewhat thin – the developers having performed a minor miracle, perhaps appropriate for such a building, in producing any photos at all. The close-up did not, however, show the hoped-for detail in the multitude of statues embedded in the wall, but the longer shot, from outside the fence, was brighter, with more sky and sun. It was mid-morning by now, the sun having only recently risen with its feeble light.

I walked around the streets in the area in front of the cathedral in order to feel some of the atmosphere of the neighbourhood, after which I performed an anti-clockwise semi-circle in order to retrace my steps the way I had come. I walked for a hundred yards, or so, to see the old bridge over the river, the Nidelva, that led up to the fort via Brubakken and Kristianbk. Brubakken was a *very* steep bank with a curious contraption at the bottom which turned out to be a

cycle lift, as I established on my return later.

I continued to the top of the bank, went to the nearest side of the fort and did a clockwise loop of the building. There were certainly good views up there. At the opposite side to which I entered, there were abundant grassy areas and a wall which overlooked the harbour area on Trondheimfjord some 1–2 km away. Families were walking their children and dogs in a place where it certainly gave the best view of the city. I descended by a slightly different route, but still managed to see and photograph the cycle lift mechanism. It required the user to place his bike in the slot on the runway, insert a coin in another slot and . . . whoosh . . . off would go the bike. Nobody used it whilst I was there. My own bike had last been seen a few years before, when I took it to the local skip, and bade it a very fond farewell.

I continued to sightsee, starting from the Very Old Bridge (called Gamle Bybro) near to the starting point of the cycle lift. The bridge was erected approximately the same time as the fort was built, around 1681. Actually, they were built after the great fire of 1681 which devastated most of medieval Trondheim. I returned by the river's side via Kjøpmannsgata towards the harbour and the patiently waiting *M/S Lofoten*. One particular shop, which was more a kiosk, near the harbour, had all sorts of goodies on view through the window. However, due to my lack of knowledge of the language, the currency, and my shyness, I did not go inside. Hopefully, my confidence would grow later.

Before boarding the boat, I took a photo of the good map of Trondheim that was displayed on a board at the quayside. We left at High Noon, so the sunlight was quite good then. On leaving the quay at Trondheim which, incidentally, is Norway's third largest town with its 135,500 inhabitants, we passed the famous Munkholmen. In the Middle Ages, Nidarholm Abbey was on this small island, but it was abandoned in 1531 after the first fire. In the 17th century it became a fortress but the canons couldn't quite reach the mainland from there – the Swedes occupied it and tried!

Both coastlines, port and starboard, were very interesting and beautiful as we made our way down the fjord. There was the Manor of Reinkloster, and the Austrat Castle further on, both to starboard. Austrat was owned by Lady Inger who ruled her property empire from there, and continued her intriguing lifestyle that involved the archbishop and many of the noblemen of the Country. The present castle is owned by the state. We first saw Austrat Castle in its forested area when heading approximately west. The boat turned left as two fjords intersect and turn us roughly south, so my eyes were kept to starboard to look at the low-lying, flat country known as Ørlandet. The radars that I could see on this rich farming land were part of the Norwegian Air Force's main air base for the county of Trondelag. The base is known as Ørland, around which we turned right and headed north with vast numbers of islands to negotiate. It was getting late as we entered the narrow, twisting Stokksund Sound which the crew skilfully navigated.

There were islands all around the craft on this magical coastline, and numerous caves in the cliffs, the best being Herkak Cave, which were often used in the past as hiding places for fugitives from the law. On the island of Stokøya,

as well as caves, there was a very good bathing beach, the best in Sør Trondelag. The best cave along this stretch of coast is Halvik Cave, at Osen, a few miles further north. This cave broadens into a lofty hall some 300 yards inside its entrance.

Whilst passing this stretch of coast, I much enjoyed the excellently presented and tasty fish lunch which we were told was Halibut. Later, I had the pleasure of seeing a beautiful sunset as 'I watched the sun go down on Stokksund Sound', rather than Galway Bay, although that tune and its lyrics were passing through my mind at the time. Sunset was at 15.48 hrs (3.48 p.m.) and this was the last full day before entering the Arctic Circle, which I calculated would be at about 07.20 hrs the next day.

Chapter V

Hitting the Aurora Trail

So I hadn't seen the Aurora Borealis as yet! It was already Saturday, 6 November and there was so much cloud on the first two nights that there was no chance. I hoped that the whole of the eleven days wouldn't get clouded off as it would be such a shocking waste of the Arctic's scenery and atmosphere not to have sightings of the Aurora. But I was getting excited about the prospects that evening if visibility was good, having never seen it before in my life, although I'd known about it since I had been a young lad.

As we approached Rørvik, having crossed the Folda, an open stretch of sea, and the third of the journey's six, we entered a narrow sound. This, the Naeroysund Sound, is between the mainland and the Vikna archipelago, and across it goes the 700m long Naeroysund Suspension Bridge, Norway's fifth largest, with a central span of 325m and 41m maximum above the water. This bridge, plus others, connect the archipelago of 6,000 islands and skerries to the mainland.

The Naeroysund Bridge was at the approach to Rørvik and it seemed to me that it would have to increase in height in order that the *Lofoten's* mast could go underneath. The 'clearance' would not be much, if any! I stood on deck with a German fellow-passenger postulating the possible 'clearance amount'. As we got closer and closer we were convinced that there would be a maximum of six inches clearance, or indeed, we might lose the mast. As we passed underneath, we could well have been right for it was certainly touch-and-go!

Looking at my data on the *Lofoten*, it gave every conceivable figure apart from the height. I could have sworn that the top ten feet, or so, were telescopically retractable, automatically coupled to a bridge-height measuring device, but how on earth would they account for the differences in sea level?

Once near Rørvik, the sky became clearer and I got excited about the Aurora possibilities. However, as soon as we docked, on came all the lights on all five decks, plus the bridge. The handling of cargo needs lots of light for reasons of safety as well as speed, especially when it was as late as 21.00 hrs and over fours hours past sunset. Not a hope in hell of seeing the sky, stars, Aurora or anything of an astronomical nature with those lights on. Even the Observation Deck was unusable for observations! Still, not to worry, this was only a short stop and we'd be moving on soon!

Like hell we would! We were three quarters of an hour late due to extra cargo loading and unloading. At last after apologies over the speakers in a variety of languages, we were on our way. These languages varied with the individual announcer, but normally all announcements included Norwegian, with English and German and sometimes French as well. If a message was for a specific person,

only his or her language would be broadcast – normally for a crew member or a passenger who was wanted for a phone call. Yes, on this *traditional* boat, one could receive and dispatch calls and faxes all over the world! From my cabin, close to Reception, I could often hear teleprinters in action.

Leaving the background lights of Rørvik, the sky got darker. Later it became apparent that some lights in the sky didn't relate to any cloud reflections from neighbouring towns. Perhaps these were the first glimpses of the Aurora, an explanation of which is as follows:

> The sun spews out ionized particles in the telescopically visible solar prominences (flares) which are associated with sunspots. These are ejected millions of miles into space and when they reach the planet Earth (which is like a giant magnet) they stream toward the north and south magnetic poles. The more sunspots there are, the more particles there are. Sunspot numbers reach a peak about every eleven years and send vast numbers of these ionized particles that reach the polar regions (north and south) with a high-level entry to the Earth's atmosphere. These particles ionize our atmosphere and produce coloured patterns of light that move randomly in the sky. It is best seen the more northerly one is in the Arctic, or more southerly in the Antarctic. These particles journey to the Earth in 20–40 hours. The illuminations are really about 60 miles, or more, above the Earth.

I could easily see something different about the Aurora compared with reflections of the town lights from particles in the sky or clouds. The green arc of light was about 120° wide with its centre at the highest altitude. That direction was approximately north, using the pole star as a reference, with the maximum elevation of about 30°. The sides of the arc were not of uniform brightness, with two parts, in particular, increasing in brightness on a random basis. The vertical extent of the green band also varied. The right-hand side would jump upwards and change colour with a small curtain-shaped area of varying colours rapidly changing its vertical extent. Then the left-hand side performed its own show of varying sizes, shapes and colours.

After watching this display, like an addictive computer game in Cinerama, I found that, in spite of the cold, I could not pull myself away from it for it seemed to have a personality of its own! It is with some appreciation that I can understand why some religious people refer to it as God's paintbrush in the sky.

I eventually pulled myself away from it at 23.10 hrs after a fantastic show that I had waited about forty years to see! It was still 6 November, and we would cross the Arctic Circle the next day at, maybe, 07.20 hrs depending on winds and tidal currents and how much of our Rørvik delay we could make up. I then bedded down for the night to prepare for this event.

I must have slept through Bronnøysund which we were scheduled to leave at 01.00 hrs, but I remember Sandnessjøen. We left there only twenty-three minutes late, at 04.38 hrs, having recovered half the time lost at Rørvik. We must have been travelling quicker and done more rapid cargo-handling. I tried to get some more sleep.

Chapter VI

Inside the Arctic Circle

On Sunday, 7 November I got rapidly out of bed at 07.20 hrs after oversleeping! I'd just missed any evidence of the 'crossing'! Sod it! I'd wanted to see the famous globe on the island at the 'crossing' point on Horseman Island (Hestmannøy), which would have been recognisable. However, after a week inside the Arctic Circle, I'd be returning on the Saturday to see these islands. So there I was, at Latitude 66°33′, and proceeding in a northerly direction, your Honour!

I learned from the crew that I'd missed the 'crossing' by a few minutes only. There wasn't a broadcast about it which was curious as I thought that there *would* have been one. Maybe I had been just too deep in sleep! I also heard from the crew that I was the only passenger making the round trip on this tour. I really felt more like Michael Palin than ever. I think that we must have had similar experiences and thoughts on our respective adventures. As distinct from mine, Michael's was designed to last for six months to allow for photography at both Poles.

It was still pre-dawn and I could see a beautiful red sky in the east over the coastal mountains many hours before sunrise. I took a photo, more in hope, with my ordinary slow film in my ordinary disk camera. It came out quite well, although not as good as the visual magic with one's own eyes. A slightly later photo that I took of a NORCARGO ship, showed only the rails of my own ship. Nothing is visible of the NORCARGO except four points of light where her on-board lights might have been. Over the following few days I saw many NORCARGO ships, terminals and facilities. NORCARGO is everywhere, it seems, and is analogous to McBraynes in the Scottish Islands.

Despite failing to add that ship to my photographic record, my relatively insensitive film did, indeed, capture the sight and atmosphere of the passing of the M/S *Finnmarken* heading south at 08.30 hrs. The pre-dawn, red skies were beautiful in their Arctic setting although to fully appreciate them is impossible with a relatively cheap film and a cheap camera. This same brought tears to my eyes, and is an experience that will live with me all my life.

As my craft neared Ørnes, we passed beautiful islands and saw wonderful views. Sunrise, in all its beauty, was at 09.50 hrs, just twenty minutes after leaving Ørnes. Earlier, I had been talking to a Swedish woman of about forty whom I'd seen before. She was an asthmatic and was just off to bed, but she said, in broken English, that she was going for a 'songing' as she likes 'songing'. I had heard her 'singing' at odd times during the two previous days, in the foyer of the ship's restaurant – but was the 'songing' really 'snogging', and where would the bed come in? I went to my cabin and had a shave, just in case! I followed the coastal details on the map as we proceeded north from Ørnes towards Bodø, where we should arrive shortly before noon. By 11.00 hrs the sun was up to about 6–7° of elevation, but by 11.35 hrs it had set behind some coastal mountains to the east. Yes, the 'sun sinks slowly in the east' in these parts, folks!

At about 11.15 hrs I saw the 'songer' with another 'songer', unmistakably in songstress's gear. Sod it! I'd wasted time having that shave! As we approached Bodø, I saw its airport built out into the fjord. Aircraft were approaching low over our craft, so we lowered our mast to let them pass with comfort. I don't know what aircraft they were, but one looked similar to a Varsity and one was similar to a Viscount. Later, a crewman expressed the view that he thought it was a military airfield and was the biggest around there. It certainly didn't look fancy enough to be a civil airport.

Having alighted from the *Lofoten* after docking at 12.30 hrs, and having taken its photo, I strode rapidly out towards the town. This meant a walk around a collection of harbour-type buildings which were alongside another road – and across a railway level crossing whose far side was blocked by a vehicle around which we all walked through rather large puddles.

Arriving at the main street, I turned right and proceeded along it going from one side of the street to the other, looking at their culture and artifacts displayed in the shops. I recall that computer diskettes were on sale at several places at prices not too dissimilar from those in the UK.

I turned up slippery, icy, side streets and through some interesting, but small, shopping precincts, retracing my way back to the boat by following a signpost which I photographed and which showed

← Tembane.hurtigrute |

and where I had to turn off for the docks.

I had left the midday meal until after my return from the streets of Bodø. The sun had already set and I settled into the comfortable corner seat in the restaurant which was mine for the whole tour. The waitress, who I later heard referred to by one of her colleagues as Edda, explained the choice. It was a fabulously prepared chicken meal, *or* an equally fabulous fish preparation. In this context the word 'or' really, means 'and' if you wanted it to! So I had some of each. And 'some' really means 'a lot'. Thus I had three chickens and two fish dishes! Both quality and quantity were terrific. I was able to finish off this vast meal before the boat hit the 'open sea' stretch across Westfjorden to the Lofoten islands. Just as well because it was a very, very choppy crossing on that leg of the journey, and I was unsure of my ability to 'keep food down' in these conditions. In the past, it hadn't been possible! This time, I wanted to use the hours of darkness of the Westfjorden crossing for observing the Aurora. We were miles from land and only the on-board lights might be a problem.

Watching the Aurora would be difficult as the sea was quite rough when we rounded the island of Landegode and then headed directly across this very wide fjord to Stamsund. We had hugged the coast until then.

The Aurora was well visible over a 60° arc centred on our heading, and at other times from 15° left of heading to 45° right of heading. To minimize the light interference with one's vision, it was best to watch from the observation area at the rear of the top-level deck.

As the boat was being tossed all over the place, the presence of a number of poles and rails made easy handholds for someone like me who wanted to concentrate on other things. The wind was strong and the temperature low, so my parka became very useful throughout this crossing. I only stopped watching the Aurora for short breaks as I had waited so long for this chance. It was only as we approached Stamsund at about 19.00 hrs that I left my position having been virtually on my own for the whole afternoon on the observation deck and in the open.

I had thus been hanging on to upright but oscillating poles from 16.30 hrs until 19.00 hrs for stabilizing my viewing position. From being a person who used to be prone to seasickness more than almost any other person on Earth, I had been transformed into an Aurora-observing automaton with piston-like legs that automatically compensated for all movements of the *Lofoten*. The sheer beauty of the Aurora, sometimes complex and active, sometimes simple and unmoving, was sufficient to divert my thoughts and mind, successfully, from the punishment of the seas.

However, during the stop at Stamsund, I went to lie down in my cabin, mainly to let my mind replay the sights I'd seen over the last few hours. A walk on firm land would probably have been difficult as my legs had now become adapted to the rolling motion of our craft.

As we moved northwards again, this time with the rugged coast of the Lofotens on our left, it was impossible to see one of the major spectacles *en route*: the sight of the Lofoten Wall. This was the penalty for not coming in the summer! The Lofoten Wall is a great sixty-mile stretch of jagged peaks. I would miss, on both outbound and inbound legs of the trip, this fabulous panorama, which I'd only seen in photographs before. It is the range of mountains after which my particular boat was named. They are composed of granite and are volcanic in origin. During the last ice-age, these mountains were subjected to severe glacial carving. Only after the glaciers disappeared did the exceptionally wild alpine grandeur appear. That night however, it had vanished again – a repeat of the problem encountered at Molde.

The next stop was Svolvaer, just one and a half hours from Stamsund. We arrived at about 21.00 hrs and I had a quick walk around exploring the streets and buildings of the town for three quarters of an hour. It was interesting to see the contents of the window displays, and compare prices with those in the UK. There was a world of difference. Doing comparisons at the prevailing exchange rate showed prices to be at least five times dearer. The town comprises predominantly clothing and bookshops! I still hadn't seen shops where one could buy large quantities of food for home-cooking! How would the housewife get on?

On returning to my cabin, I planned my logistics and photography for the remainder of the trip, now knowing the hours of daylight and the height of the sun this far north. Many towns would remain unphotographed as I would see so few in daylight. Photographic plans would now be concentrated around scenes from on board whilst sailing during the hours of daylight. That would be far better, I reckoned, than just getting dark photos of buildings however interesting they might have been by day. I thus marked my chart (a specially modified version of Annex A) with possible photo-opportunities until the end of the expedition.

On leaving Svolvaer, and before visiting the Trolls in their own fjord, the vessel seemed intent on finding the biggest waves in the remaining areas of open water. The sky was clear on this stretch so there would be the chance to Aurora-watch. However, I left that until the calm of the Trollfjord. Unfortunately, on entering the fjord through its narrow entrance, the cloud cover was too high in the

Aurora's direction, so after a busy and exhausting day it was time to a rest in my cabin.

The overnight journey taking us into 8 November was quite pleasant. It was through an offshore fjord system in Vesteralen, north of the Lofotens, and the fact that the boat did not roll made the overnight trip very agreeable. However, in the approaches to Stockmarknes, a howling wind could be heard inside my cabin. It sounded really bad, but the ship was still not rolling, and the view from my porthole revealed a calmly gliding scene. The night stops at Sortland and Risoyhamn could be witnessed only by moving the venetian blind near my bed.

Arriving at Harstad I hoped to visit and photograph parts of the town before breakfast, so I had a quick 'wash and dress' and went out with my camera to Harstad itself. I inspected the dockside quickly before moving on to the coach station, the shops, houses and an estate. Everywhere I saw snow, shovelled to the edges of the roads in piles, as I wandered around trying to get the feel of the town, its people and the Norwegian way of life.

Sunrise didn't occur before the boat sailed at 08.00 hrs and it would be quite a while before it did. I had arrived back at the *Lofoten* at that time, expecting an 08.15 hrs departure, but I was greeted by the 'BONG, BONG' which heralded announcements over the tannoy. Essentially, it was ' . . . we are now leaving Harstad'. Who's a lucky boy, then? I had been using a slightly out-of-date timetable, which, until now, had shown no variations. Hereafter, I would pay attention to the board displayed near the gang-plank; just before each arrival this gave the actual proposed departure time for the place in question.

I had breakfast at my normal restaurant table. The sun,

which I had waited for so long to see illuminate the streets of Harstad, seemed still unwilling to rise. During breakfast, I had the pleasure of the fantastic Arctic pre-dawn scene of lovely reds with clouds illuminated from their undersides. This beauty was accentuated by the sky behind the silhouetted mountains and with the waters of the fjord in the foreground. There was even a new fraulein at breakfast to improve the internal scenery!

Later, I strolled around the decks before sunrise in a pullover and a Russian-style hat. The *Lofoten* was gently drifting along the fjord with snow-clad mountains all around. Except for the lowest 150 feet or so, the snow completely covered these mountains. It produced a beautiful inner feeling that no camera could portray. How does one record the feelings encountered? I did not see the actual sunrise. It sneaked up on us by emerging from behind a cloud situated behind a mountain at about 10.30 hrs. At last, I could now see the scenery that I'd been waiting for so long to see – many fjords, some wide, others narrower – mostly bigger than I had imagined!

I talked with a crewman on the *Lofoten* who introduced himself as Karl, so I told him that I was Roy. What a coincidence, he mused, as standing by him was a colleague with the same name! We became good friends for the whole trip.

It was late morning as the boat approached the impressive, typically Norwegian, concrete bridge at Finnsnes. Actually the town and harbour turned up before the bridge. Sneaky!! The just-over-half-hour stop at Finnsnes saw me being brave, just like at Trondheim. Here, though, I was more confident with my exploration – up the hill, across the roundabout towards town, along the main and side streets, car parks, window-shopping, general around-town viewing and sightseeing. It was more a large village than a town. It was here that I bought my first items in a Norwegian shop – a supply of goodies to eat and drink on board. They were more expensive than in the UK, but cheaper than the nearest equivalent items sold on board the *Lofoten*. Fizzy drinks, including 'Solo', were among my purchases. They supplemented my haute cuisine over the next few days. I really was eating too much! The low-calorie, low-sugar drinks shouldn't be too bad!

I really enjoyed the walk around Finnsnes which seemed like hours to me – a welcome break from the small on-board entourage! It was great! Now we were heading north again, under the Finnsnes Bridge, for an afternoon visit to Tromsø where we would stop for over three hours! Whoopee!! Before leaving the delightful Finnsnes, I took some photos as we approached and went underneath the bridge, which, at 1,150 metres in length and joining Finnsnes and Senja, is one of the longest pillar-bridges in Europe. It is something special!

As we headed approximately north – the actual heading at any time varied according to our position in the network of fjords that we were in – the scenery got even better and more photos were taken in the low light, along the Gisund Sound and left into Balsfjord. This was what I had hoped to see. This was what the trip had been for. Better still, lunch was now being served – I had Codfish served the special Norwegian way – and I could enjoy the fabulous views from my window in the restaurant. It was a wonder that I didn't get indigestion from jumping up and down to look through the windows on the opposite side. I was just like a silly schoolboy, but loving every moment of it.

The snowy peaks bordering these two fjords were *my* idea of the *real* coast of Norway, and they drifted slowly by at 15 m.p.h. It was a fantastic feeling.

We arrived in Tromsø close to dusk, so I went ashore to see the fabulously modern architecture of the Ice Cathedral, just across the fjord. However, it meant crossing the very large bridge to get to the cathedral on the far side, three quarters of an hour from the *Lofoten*. That bridge was LONG! The view behind the Ice Cathedral, when seen from its front, reminded me of the one from Interlaken towards the Jungfrau. The valley and scenery were so similar.

Having got close to the Ice Cathedral, which is not actually made of ice, I discovered that it was too late – now 15.30 hrs – to take photographs. However, the sights and atmosphere of the place, its surroundings, its people, the *feelings* and so on, compensated for the lack of photos. The view during the walk back to the *Lofoten*, in the dark, was a beautiful vista of light – no wonder it is called the Paris of the North!

On returning to my cabin, I wrote letters to friends in the UK. While the boat was leaving the port, I talked with a very good friend on board. I will call him the 'Oslo Geordie' in this account as I never got to know his name. We talked about our respective travels. He had made many more than I had done – for two reasons. Firstly, he was older and retired. Secondly, he spent his working life in Norwegian shopping industry, and had clearly been around the world a few times. He came from Oslo, where he still lives, and spoke very good English with a Geordie accent. His seven years as a resident of Newcastle on Tyne gave him that distinctive version of the English language, and he was quite fluent. When I had asked him earlier 'which Newcastle?' he had replied that for Norwegians, especially seafaring ones, there was only one Newcastle. You may recall, from reading Chapter Two, that this link between the UK and Norway is still very much alive today. One either flies from Heathrow, as I did, or sails from Newcastle.

Our departure from Tromsø was at about 06.00 hrs, so the 'Oslo Geordie' and I chatted on deck as we plied our way along the Balsfjord, observing all the lights on both sides. I never saw as much light in Norway, before or since, as during that evening with the old and new Tromsøs on either side of the fjord. We watched the university halls of residence glide by and I learned a lot of the background of this town and its changes from my friend that evening. In the middle of the fjord there was the island of Tromsøy, upon which was built the urban centre of Tromsø. That urban centre contained a third of the inhabitants, a further third being in the suburbs whilst the rest were in the outlying areas, making Norway's largest urban community, covering 960 square miles including fishing villages, farmland and reindeer pastures.

Apart from being known as the 'Paris of the North', its other title is 'Capital of the Arctic'. As the scenery became darker, I was able to renew my Aurora-watching activities. I had my fourth session of observations and later, my fifth, where it extended to 150° of arc. Rising elements from the main band were quite a feature.

It had been quite a day as I retired to my cabin on the night of 8 November.

Chapter VII

I meet my Love
or
On Top of the world

Clanking chains and other sounds awaken me on this, a very special morning. The noises originate from outside the cabin's porthole and it passed through my mind that we might have pulled in early for repairs after a stormy night. But it is just an early arrival at Hammerfest, the world's most northerly city at a latitude of more than 70°. We had obviously already called at Skjervoy and Oksfjord whilst I'd been asleep, departures being scheduled from these places at 22.30 hrs and 02.00 hrs.

I got dressed in a C&W shirt and went out on deck to investigate. It was OK! It was Hammerfest, or so the sign on the harbour said. I had a five-minute walk around a small bit of town, but found it very cold on streets unprotected from even the low-speed easterly wind. The chill-factor made it the coldest place that I'd been to in my life. I loved it. I returned to the *Lofoten* and my cabin to warm my 'inside' with the cafeteria's beautiful hot chocolate drink and chocolate cakes. We would be in Hammerfest from 05.30 hrs until 08.00 hrs. Music in the cafeteria wasn't exactly Country Music, but it was certainly easy-listening

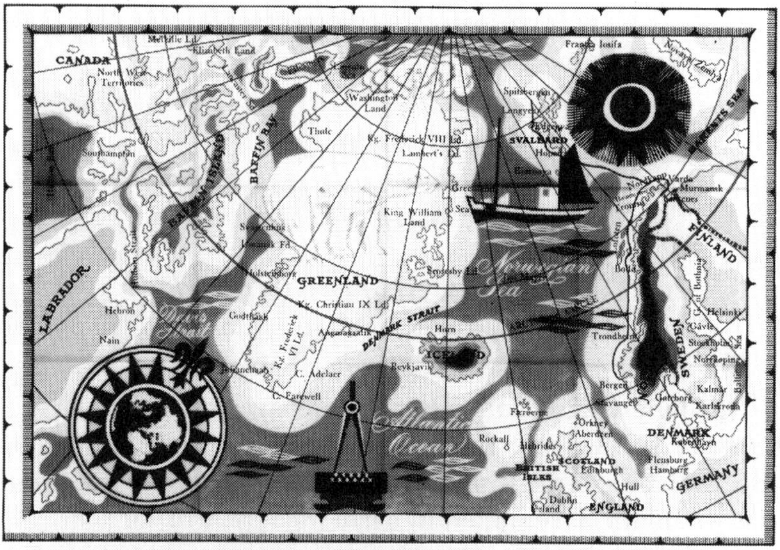

POLARSIRKEL-SERTIFIKAT

Certificate of Arctic Circle / Zertifikat für das Passieren des Polarkreises / Certificat du Cercle Polaire Arcticque

Jeg, Njord, Gud over de 7 hav, gjør hermed vitterlig at

I, Njord God of all the Seas, hereby give witness that / Ich, Njord, Gott über alle Meere, tue hiermit kund / Nous, Njord, Dieu de tous les océans, attestons que

ROY PETERS

om bord på M/S «Lofoten» av Finnmark Fylkesrederi og Ruteselskap

On board the ship of Finnmark Fylkesrederi og Ruteselskap / An bord des Schiffes der Finnmark Fylkesrederi og Ruteselskap / A bord du navire de la Finnmark Fylkesrederi og Ruteselskap

passerte Polarsirkelen, den 7/11-93

Crossed the Arctic Circle / Überquerte den Polarkreis / A passé le Cercle Polaire Arcticque.

Måtte hell og lykke følge deg på denne reise og for all fremtid.

May good luck and happiness follow you on this voyage and an ever / Möge Glück und Segen Sie auf dieser Reise und ewiglich begleiten! / Nous vous souhaitons bon voyage et une vie heureuse.

Hestmannøy, 7/11 1993

Kaptein/Captain/Kapitän/Commandant

M/S LOFOTEN FFR 07 NOV. 1993 POLARSIRKELEN

in style. There were bands and a lovely predominantly piano instrumental version of 'Ain't she sweet!'

I redressed myself in the parka which had been waiting for that sort of temperature since I'd bought it some years before. It was still two hours until we sailed and had breakfast – and four to five hours until sunrise. Not only the parka would be used for the coming walk, but also the Russian-type hat and the newly purchased thermal gloves. They would be very comfortable.

Clad in these garments, I left the boat and immediately fell in love with the town. It was real holiday weather – not the oppressive oven-type temperature that people *say* they enjoy in the Mediterranean. Those sort of temperatures are HELL, whereas this is for real people – nice fresh air and so comfortable, and such a beautiful place! I saw a cinema advert for Chuck Norris and the *Texas Rangers*, a Country & Western film showing locally. This was a coincidence because the first club that I joined in the UK for *live* Country Music was the Texas Rangers (Frontier Post) at West Malvern.

The heat of Texas (!) was moderated by the strong wind-chill factor as I passed the Ekspedisjon shop on the corner. Unfortunately, I wouldn't be going on to the North Pole, but I could always stock up at this shop if I wanted. But unfortunately it was not yet opening time. The hooded parka protected me wonderfully from the strong, driving wind from the east. It was not a sea breeze any more, not a gentle gift from the Gulf Stream! Looking at the Chuck Norris film advert, you would think that it should be Alaska rather than TEXAS. Alaska! Hell No!! We ain't as far south as those guys – and we are heading further north soon!

This was the right place for a parka, hat and gloves – the

first time that I'd felt comfortable in the parka since I bought it all those years before.

I now had a long walk around town and found St Michael's church, a lovely, modern-looking building with unique architecture as seen in all the brochures. Sadly it was too dark for photos but I'd catch it on the way back. I did take one photo of the Ekspedisjon shop but was not worried by the lack of light since the lighting of the shop-signs would be adequate, and it proved to be so when the film was developed.

As we left and the boat plied its way towards the North Pole, or North Cape to be more precise, tears welled up in my eyes for my sheer love of the place. Songs ran through my mind which I would forever associate with Hammerfest, such as:

'South to Alaska'
(to the tune of 'North to Alaska')

'Leaving of Hammerfest'
(to the tune of 'Leaving of Liverpool')

'I love Hammerfest in Winter'
(to the tune of 'I love Paris in the Springtime')

I felt really at home there. No one complained about the cold – they just got on with their lives in the cool, fresh air. In the intense cold, people walked to work or took their leisure without hats! Never mind, I'd be back in two days' time.

On the way north, I spoke to the crewman, Roy, about my love of Hammerfest. He explained that he and his family felt the same way. The company that operated the *Lofoten* had its headquarters there too. Roy told me about the Ice Bear Club, in Hammerfest, which his whole family had joined. My own library books and other references even mentioned the club, which anyone could join, be they a small child with parent (as in my friend Roy's case) or His Majesty, King Harald of Norway, who in fact did join. The only condition was that one must apply *in person* to the Town Hall in Hammerfest. I had already seen the place on my walk, and noticed the two full-sized models of polar bears outside. I spoke with Roy at length, whilst he was marking up my Hammerfest map with interesting places, which we then discussed. On my return two day's later, I decided that I would become a member of the club and also photograph the charming St Michael's Church.

I also spoke to Roy about the operators of our boat, their headquarters, what the company was like and how things had changed following the amalgamation of five shipping companies through a sort of nationalization. It had been the NSR (Norwegian State Railways) people who provided me with the overall timetables, documentation, arrangements etc. The companies still ran as separate entities, but were well integrated with their operations. He said that it gave the employees a better sense of purpose and an incentive to do the job with pride, thereby making it better for the customers. Customers and crew ate and joked together creating a real classless society with everybody becoming good friends, enjoying working and relaxing together. Some members of the crew could not always eat with us because they worked in the canteen, cargo handling, cookhouse or offices and ate on the job, which they loved. Sometimes, however, when off-duty, they would join us.

Our next port-of-call was Havoysund, a short stop, leaving at 11.00 hrs. We were now in the channels near the most northerly point of Europe. I went for a short walk to stretch my legs, turning right on to the coast road, the mountains to my left, the sea down below to the right. I couldn't go far, but I'd wanted to see as much as possible other than the shops on this occasion. I greeted several people with cheery 'Hallos' especially on the way back, meeting a woman of about thirty summers, and doubtless the same number of winters, with her playful, large, fluffy dog, a beautiful hairy husky. My TV memories of these animals were of the sled-pulling, bionic wonder dogs of *The Iditerod Trail.* This lady's dog was an altogether 'human' type of fun-loving canine pet which changed my view of huskies completely!

Our boat moved off after we had all reboarded and others had got on. I settled down to a chocolate drink from the push-button machine and paid for it at the counter for 13.00Kr. I also felt very much at home at this last stop, and indeed the whole area felt like somewhere I'd like to live in. At noon as we entered a channel just south of NordKapp, the sun was at only 1.5° in the sky even at midday. The reason we can go south of North Cape is that the Cape is on an island about seven miles by eight in size. This far north I am still able to take photos, clad only in trousers and a blue C&W shirt.

Whilst rounding the south-east corner of NordKapp I could see various signs of habitation in coves and in valleys, with terraced lawns of snow and maybe vegetables. There were about a dozen houses in one bay which I photographed.

Later, I saw what may have been Honningsvag but half

an hour early. On commenting about this to a crew member, he said, 'Yes, we have very good wind – get here quick!' He had been my original receptionist, rather than Roy who spoke better English. I quickly changed into my parka and other gear more appropriate to a North Cape landing. This was to be our most northerly point of call, the small town of Havoysund, which was even further north than Hammerfest, the worlds's most northerly city.

Chapter VIII

North Cape and Russia

I left *Lofoten* in the harbour and followed the delightful streets of Honningsvag on the North Cape. We were now up to 71° North (at 26° East) and just 1,311 miles from the North Pole, or so it said at the harbour entrance. The roads and pavements were very icy and there was much compacted snow about. It must have been dangerous driving in such conditions but the inhabitants were obviously very skilled, motoring as fast there as *we* do on clear roads. The conditions obviously give them marvellous opportunities for rally practice!

Walking as carefully as possible on the slippery surface I wandered around town soaking up the atmosphere of the place. I looked at shops, housing estates and later, mountains and snow. Seeing one house, I thought 'That guy's either had an avalanche in his garden, or been very busy with a spade!' Due to our early arrival, I had longer there than expected and could thus enjoy the cold beauty of that very northerly town on the island of North Cape. Because of the icy pavements, however, I felt it prudent it walk on the roads. Norwegians, I noticed, always face the oncoming traffic in these situations, much more so than we British. I was amongst like-minded people. It was quite an experience seeing oncoming traffic, travelling at high throttle settings, heading directly for you, but avoiding you by their pure driving skills on ice.

As I was running short of film for my camera, I started to look for somewhere to get more. When I failed to get the right film for a disc camera in one shop I was told that the place I should try was 400 metres away and was called 'Photoland', but I was unable to find it in either direction on the main road or the many side streets.

Now I needed to hurry for two reasons. Firstly, there was the late midday meal, and secondly, sunset was imminent. I had to be aware of the icy pavements and the need to share the roads with oncoming rally drivers in the fading light. It was well past lighting-up time at 13.00 hrs. Thus I arrived, in the dark, back at the *Lofoten*, twenty-five minutes late for the start of the midday lunch. But that was OK! As ever, the fish was both excellent and substantial, and afterwards I relaxed before the trip to our next port-of-call at Kjollefjord.

That turned out to be the worst leg of the journey to date. It was very rough and the craft pitched and rolled all the way until the last few minutes before docking at Kjollefjord, which was sheer heaven! I disembarked for a short walk because, although not actually sick, I wasn't feeling too good. It was a nice little place with heavily compacted snow and ice. Although it was only a short stop, I can still recall the charming calmness of the water beside the towering rocks as we entered and departed from that port. It was in the half-light and was in such contrast to the open sea.

One of my friends among the crew told me that strong winds were forecast for our next, overnight leg. They would be from the South and far stronger than what we had just endured, so he offered me some pills. Nice man! Despite my previous problems with travel sickness, which I related to him, I said that I believed that I had now overcome them and was able to decline his very kind offer. Two wide fjords ran north-south so would not protect us much as we passed their mouths. We'd had the same problem on the previous leg with the Porsangerfjord and the Laksefjord.

The next stage would obviously be even less pleasant on the stomach, so from Kjollefjord to Mehamn I relaxed on the bed in my cabin with my eyes closed, whatever the boat did, trying as much as possible not to move, or to obtain any visual cues, so as to prevent my system being upset. On that leg of the journey, they provided me with an excellent evening meal of reindeer and other meats of a savory nature. Reindeer, itself, has a fantastic taste, this being the first time that I'd experienced it – rather like a beef taste with the texture of pork – similar to swordfish, which I've had twice in twenty-five years. So reindeer is a 'bully' version of swordfish! I didn't actually eat during that sea-leg, but waited until we tied up at Mehamn, our most northerly point on the journey, at around 20.00 hrs. This precaution avoided any potential travel-sickness problems.

Mehamn had the inevitable NORCARGO terminal which *everywhere* along the coast seemed to have, this one containing a good number of Arctic Cats (Snowmobiles) and a selection of arctic camping and survival gear, which many places in that part of the world seem to have.

Once again I relaxed on the next leg to avoid sickness from the peculiar motions of the boat. Arriving at Berlevag I saw that it was only big lump of concrete in the middle of nowhere, at the end of a long breakwater. There was very little of interest to see but at least it was different, so I went for a short walk before returning to my cabin for the night.

I awoke in the early morning at 05.10 hrs from the clattering of leaving the dock at Vardo. I hadn't even been awakened by our arrival – which I might have expected. I had clearly slept through our arrival and departure from Batsfjord, which would have been around 01.00 hrs. It was now 10 November and on that day our boat would reach its halfway distance and turning point at Kirkenes. It was the next stop later that morning, and only three miles from the border with Russia!

I went off to sleep again and reawoke at 08.10 hrs whilst approaching Kirkenes. The snow on the mountains to our right seemed to come right down to the sea. Well, not quite, as it only comes down to the high tide level, anything lower being melted away by the comparatively warmer sea. So there were a few feet of bare rocks above the sea to the lowest snow – the most level snowline that I've seen in my life!

As there was about an hour and a half for the scheduled stop, I quickly had breakfast before my short walk into town from the docks, which I did in a country & western shirt. 'The End of the Trail' is appropriate for Kirkenes. It really is 'the end of the trail' as this is the furthest point along the coast that we visit from Bergen, and is only three miles from the Russian border. Given more time, I could have walked into Russia and back. It was only a short trek across the frozen tundra. After passing a car from the USA, an 'Armbruster Stageway' Buick, which on closer inspection turned out to be a hearse, I headed off towards Russia, joining the main road to town from the link road to the docks. I noticed how skilled the drivers of vehicles were in the icy conditions. At a collection of shacks and shops, signposted 1.5 km to town, after surveying the situation, I reluctantly headed back towards the *Lofoten*, returning on the opposite side of the road where I witnessed a sight to remember for the rest of my life – an old lady pushing a pram-ski-Zimmer frame contraption.

I rapidly crossed the road in the poor light to get a closer glimpse, and one of my feet sank six inches deep through the crust of the snow which, in retrospect, was probably the edge of the pavement. But I hurried on, as I was too interested in seeing the 'vehicle' being pushed by the old lady. It was like a Zimmer frame, but was on skis, and she had shopping on top of it. What a crafty design, I thought.

On questioning my 'Oslo-Geordie' friend about this on my return, he told me that it's a common sight in Norway and he drew me what he thought I had described. Where the old woman had her shopping, he said, younger women often carry a child to the shops. It was normally called a *Sparkstotting*. I was to witness this mode of shopping later in the trip, and indeed on TV after my return especially during the Winter Olympics at Lillehammer.

I chatted with 'Oslo Geordie' all the way from Kirkenes to Vadso where we arrived at 11.45 hrs approximately, which meant that leg was entirely in daylight for a change! It was a pleasant journey across Varanger Fjord. Geordie proved to be an intelligent man who had retired from the shipping industry. We spoke on a number of subjects on this leg of the journey, including computers, education and places that we'd both visited in our lives. He had a Compac 486 computer at home, having retired just over ten years previously from his job of developing techniques to improve the shipping industry. He'd heard overnight on the radio about a Russian trawler that had caught fire in the area, and he pointed it out to me. He was a very interesting companion, not only on this particular stage but on our many meetings over the several days of our acquaintance.

I walked on my own, as usual, around Vadso, with its skilful drivers negotiating the compacted ice and snow around town. Not so much a town as a coastal village from what I saw of it, with the snow being treacherous especially for walking the steep slopes, but it was an interesting walk. I had to be back at the boat by 12.15 hrs, but took some photographs and met two girls from the boat doing the same thing in the failing light. I doubted whether their flash photos would come out as the sun had already set! There were attractive houses, and some very interesting views in the direction of a bay with its surface almost completely frozen over with ice.

Back on the boat, my crewman friend, Roy, told me that the two girls were working in the kitchens and elsewhere in a training capacity gaining work experience on board our craft.

Midday lunch, that Wednesday, was a wonderfully prepared meal of lamb. The continuous high quality of the food, its preparation and its taste were something to marvel at.

By mid-afternoon we found ourselves arriving at Vardo where we had about an hour's stop. In retrospect, it seemed like several hours because I had two walks, returning to the boat in between. It was the first time that I did some supermarket shopping in Norway – just as I was beginning to think that they didn't exist! Sure enough, young women had children and shopping on their *sparkstottings*. One man was even giving his lads a faster ride around the streets as if they were in a race. It was really pleasant, although the sun had already set. My supermarket shopping would soon fill the cupboards in my cabin, not that I would be hungry with all the marvellous fare in the restaurant at meal times. That shopping trip was on my first walk, the return to the boat being to put on my 'treaded' walking boots because of all the snow and ice.

On the second walk, I went mainly in the other direction, although I did return to the Shell station near the supermarket in an attempt to buy a film for my camera as I had no more left.

Back in the boat after failing to buy any film, we were now on the leg of the journey to Batsfjord during which I enjoyed more conversations with the 'Oslo Geordie'

My boat left Vardo at about 16.30 hrs and set off on the 3-hour leg to Batsfjord. It provided me with the necessary banking facilities, especially the cashing of traveller's cheques. I decided on another £40 worth, which purchased 412 Kroner. One hour out, I noticed a single band of Aurora, and had a further chat with my Geordie mate from Oslo before sorting out the shopping that I'd bought in Vardo.

I had missed Batsfjord on the way north as it had been the middle of the night, so there would be a better chance of seeing it at 19.30 hrs on our return. More than that, it turned out to be a delightful port area leading to the fishing village of Batsfjord. It was a case of up and down the icy slopes, impossible to drive them in England but simple for Norwegians! The two girls that I'd seen in Vadso were again photographing each other with flash cameras in the poor light.

Back on board again, my preference was for the pleasure of another exotic fish dinner in the restaurant. This had been prepared in a fantastic way. Being rather indulgent, I then progressed to a delicious pork schnitzel topped with a small fish in oil, and I even had a second helping of that!

After such a gastronomic evening I went up on deck for a quick look at the Aurora display. Then after a rest period in my cabin I returned for more of the Aurora. Unfortunately it was less impressive than before but on speaking with the Captain, who'd seen marvellous displays many times in his life, I learned that the spectacle earlier that evening had been a 'very special one – very impressive'.

At Berlevag (21.30–22.00 hrs) again, and we were there earlier in the day than on the previous occasion (at 01.30 hrs) less than forty-eight hours earlier. I stayed in my cabin because I was so unimpressed visually with the great *block of concrete in the sea* last time. It was enough to have walked it just the once. In earlier years, people would have had to transfer to small boats to visit the place. From 1975, a solution was sought by building a breakwater which was subsequently smashed by storms on two occasions. Their current solution is *tetrapods* which are huge concrete blocks varying in size from fifteen to twenty-five tons which have since survived thirty-foot waves. It could be *rough* there, for in 1882, every single fishing boat was sunk by a storm, and it happened again this century. Despite, or because of, these stories, I stayed in my cabin.

I went to sleep but woke up at 23.28 hrs in mid-voyage to Mehamn. Off to sleep again, with a further awakening at 00.37 hrs accompanied by tyre-screeching outside the windows. No! We had not arrived at Silverstone on a practice-day – it indicated our docking at Mehamn. Since it was calm there, I ate and drank some of my on-board refreshments from the Vardo supermarket. After that, I tried to get to sleep again, but failed to do so between

Mehamn and Kjollefjord, but at least it was a rest. The back of my neck was perspiring far too much for comfort or sleep.

Our vessel arrived at Kjollefjord at 03.15 hrs on Thursday, 11 November, and I could see through the slats in the blinds on the cabin window, that although there was no snow or ice on the harbour roads, there were piles of it along their sides. I had a snack in my cabin to keep me going over the next few hours of the journey to Honningsvag on North Cape. I ate *then* because that leg crossed the mouths of two fjords and the boat would obviously be adversely affected by the strong southerly winds blowing out of them. After that, 03.32 hrs, the boat was ready for take-off and I settled down for another short sleep. I wished myself 'goodnight' and the next thing I knew was that we were arriving at Honingsvag at 05.45 hrs. This was the first time that I'd arrived at a place in Norway already knowing the town's layout!

I got washed and dressed with eager anticipation and then explored the place further than I had done last time on 9 November. Not only did I go further but I took more interest in the houses, their window displays and the contents of the shops. Their window displays are more like those in the Netherlands, but I wondered whether the reasons were the same. There is also an undue excess of Barbie Dolls. For all the exploration I was still unable to find Photoland and some disc film that I so urgently needed for my camera.

On returning to my cabin to change into 'indoor gear', I enquired whether we would go the other, northerly way round North Cape on the way back. I was told that we would follow the same channels because of winter although they sometimes go the other way in summer. This crewman told me that there was insufficient time in our current schedule to go 'the long way round' the island. To another person, whilst on a walk, my cheery 'Good Morning' was responded to by a hearty 'God Morgen'. As we left Honningsvag at 06.45 hrs and there was a long wait until breakfast in the restaurant, I went along to the cafeteria, arriving in my blue country & western *End of the Trail* shirt. This time, the music included 'John Brown's Body' with Norwegian lyrics. After I'd finished my chocolate drink, a new number to me, then, called 'Stand and Deliverance' with English lyrics, but with neither an English singer nor an English speaking DJ.

On the south-east and south coast of Nord Kapp, the snow was all the way down to sea level with terraced and cultivated slopes. Breakfast time arrived and, still in my C&W shirt, I listened to more good music, although I could not understand the lyrics and didn't know the tunes. One of the songs a bit later sounded like 'Here I go down that wrong road again' with a voice not unlike the Irish singer Philomena Begley. The next song was a Country one as well, but I only understood two words: '. . . in Tennessee'. It was sung in a perky voice, very similar in style to the great Dolly Parton's.

These sounds caressed my ears as the beautiful North Cape drifted past the boat. Good music for good scenery, which equates to heaven, or something appreciably better! Back in my cabin on the other (south) side of the boat one deck lower, I could see the beautiful, pre-dawn, red sky which formed a fantastic backdrop to the foreground mountains of the mainland. It was just 08.30 hrs. The headwind, or perhaps an opposing sea current, was making us late for

Havoysund. Whilst waiting in the foyer to the lounge, I listened to a fabulous 'Country Rock' song by Jacobsen. Norway, if indeed it was Norwegian, would get a runaway win in the Eurovision Song contest if they chose to enter that one! It was a great number which I'd never heard before and would 'go down a bomb' in any dance hall too.

On reaching Havoysund, there was only time for a five-minute walk for a quick look in the opposite direction to that which I took the previous time on 9 November. Back on deck, I met a new friend, a man who wanted to practise his already very good English. He was a chatty, friendly person who came from the local area. He fishes around the islands off Havoysund, had been to London many times on business and told me a lot about the character, habits and customs of this very northern area. He confirmed that the current was against us and said that an 8-knot opposing current could play havoc with the speed of a 15-knot boat.

The sun was getting higher now, at three quarters of a degree above the horizon. Every day we saw another boat of the combined fleet of eleven vessels, each one heading in the opposite direction to ourselves!

The *Ragnvald Jarl* passed on the port side that day, a boat of similar vintage and size to our own. Ours was built in 1964 and the other one in 1956. Both were rebuilt in 1985 and have 4–6 car spaces which are hardly ever used this time of year.

By 11.06 hrs the sun had risen to one and three quarters of a degree in elevation! Earlier, at 10.15 hrs, the porthole acted as a pinhole camera. The opposite wall of my cabin had two 'pictures' produced by the low-angled sun. The lower 'picture' was the sun shining directly through the porthole whilst the upper one was a moving picture produced by low-angle reflections from the waves on the sea. The moving picture was intriguing in contrast to the lower, static one. But Hammerfest was getting closer and I was now getting more and more excited.

Chapter IX

The Ice Bear Club

Preparing to arrive at Hammerfest, I wanted to do three things: first and foremost to visit the Polar Bear Society building; secondly, I wanted to photograph the unusual St Michael's church; thirdly, I wanted to replenish my stock of film, now running low despite the long hours of daytime darkness.

The boat arrived three quarters of an hour late at Hammerfest's quay, and therefore I had to move quickly as it meant that the stop would only be for an hour. I walked excitedly to the Polar Bear Society building, a special room in the town hall, became a member and took a photo outside their entrance. Whilst inside the club's enrolment room, I wandered around their interesting exhibition of stuffed polar animals. They included not only bears and arctic foxes but all manner of creatures from these frozen parts. On becoming a member, I received a membership card, stickers for cars and windows, an assortment of paperwork and, it appears, most people's favourite item, a polar bear badge for one's jacket or coat. My own favourite items were my membership card and the certificate of membership.

I then progressed along Kirkegata, having left Sjbgata, and headed uphill to the wonderful modern church of St Michael's. Despite it being midday, the sun was still very low and the light was not good for an ordinary, non-specialist disc-camera with ordinary film. The problem was compounded by the sun quickly setting behind a mountain.

I progressed some way beyond the church, then down the hill again, looking all the time for photographic shops, or their equivalents, which might sell disc films. No one, not even Kodak agents, had them or even knew about them. It had been the same in all towns in the last couple of days or more. Whilst visiting these shops I searched my pockets, and noticed that I had lost my membership card for the Polar Bear Society. I went back to each shop but it had not been handed in.

Back on the boat, I needed to do two things – firstly to find a means of getting a replacement membership card, and secondly to try and get a disc film for my disc camera. The waitress arranged for me to see the Chief Steward to obtain the film and I provided him with an actual sample of the box that it came in. He said that his contacts would ensure that he'd have one for me the next day and the cost would be 45Kr.

Our arrival at Oksfjord (not Oxford) was late. This was not due to 'leaves on the line' but to headwinds and head-currents. It wasn't the last stop before Paddington either! Some couples disembarked with their prams and their offspring. One lady and a dog, whose legs were only just longer than the depth of the snow, made their excited way ashore. By contrast, one dog got on with legs 'as high as an elephant's eye' (I quote). He proceeded to take his 'keeper' to the 3rd floor lounge of the *Lofoten*, not understanding the sign restricting dogs there. But with his size, who was going to tell him?

Because we were so far behind time arriving at Oksfjord, we only had a ten-minute stop there for getting the essential unloading of cargo done, plus the loading of some other freight. Then we were on our way to Skjervoy, a leg lasting three hours. Although we were one hour late at this point, the evening meal still went ahead on time.

I told myself to 'have a kip now, lad' as I had got up early enough the previous night, and early enough that morning. The fact that the sun set at noon was curious to say the least! That evening, I saw no Aurora although I had high hopes of doing so and had three dinners between 19.00 and 20.00 hrs. There was an unusually different, exciting fish cake, far different from the humdrum UK equivalent of the same name. There was also a somewhat different chicken curry, and then a beautiful salad. What fantastic food there was on that floating, travelling restaurant! After we pulled into Skjervoy, I went for a short walk from 20.00 hrs with a Norwegian with whom I had a very interesting chat.

It was a nice little village neatly moulded around the harbour. I was so glad to have seen it, as I had missed it on the journey northwards, that being a 22.30 hrs stop after the exciting time in Tromsø earlier. After leaving Skjervoy, I filled in the NSR questionnaire about the trip. I was hoping to witness the Aurora later, but it was not to be seen. The day had been so eventful that, being so tired and happy, I lay down on my bed fully clothed and fell asleep.

Chapter X

Getting sorted out in Sortland (It's Double Dutch!)

After a good sleep I was awakened by the inevitable clanking of chains and the like. My watch told me that the time was 01.50 hrs and, on drawing the blinds aside, I recognized the unmistakable Ice Cathedral of Tromsø across the river. This wasn't the arrival, but our departure! We were undocking. The lights of Tromsø, so unusual in Norway, reminded me why it had acquired its tag of 'Paris of the North'. The bridge that I had taken so long to find and cross on the northerly leg of our journey, the cathedral, the atmosphere of the place, all brought back and rekindled in a split second the marvellous memories of a few days ago. Unfortunately, I had been asleep this time and could not relive these memories ashore – I would have to be content with a mental and emotional replay as we headed south. Farewell Tromsø!

I left the curtains drawn back and the venetian blinds angled open as we pulled out. I contentedly indulged in the beautiful sight of this lovely place as Tromsø drifted silently away. As I had a little snack I could not help giving an emotional, romantic wave of farewell to this 'Paris of the North'. Time for bed, so I got undressed, this time acknowledging that it really was night-time and went back to sleep again, this time on purpose! However, I awoke between 05.25 and 05.35 hrs with absolutely no view from my own porthole, so I dozed off again.

On reawakening at about 07.30 hrs, I washed, got dressed and went for a walk on deck in preparation for the arrival at Harstad. We arrived very late there after I had obviously slept through Finnsnes, but I spoke with a woman whose dog was taking her for a walk as its poop-scooping assistant! I later spoke with a man in his late twenties who had lived there for twelve months. He told me about this lovely place but said, nevertheless, that he was moving to Lillehammer with his job, even before the winter Olympics people moved in, but he was really from Trondheim and proud of it.

I walked around Harstad on a different route to my first visit there – and all this before breakfast. The pre-dawn views were stunning but there was not enough light for photography. At breakfast, I made conversation with one of a pair of ladies on the next table – they obviously weren't English but we conversed in English. She said that, like me, she preferred these nice 'little' boats because there was 'no atmosphere' on the larger ones.

When they were talking to each other their conversation was not intelligible to me, but it was, nevertheless, interesting for it didn't appear to be Norwegian. What those two young ladies said to each other included such English-sounding phrases as 'Lieken Shafting?' with the response 'Bien shafted!' As I say, I don't know what that language was or what it meant – but it certainly sounded interesting!

At breakfast, my waitress delivered the promised photo-disc to the table and later I would be able to take a few more photographs of the mountains to the north of the channel in which we were travelling, west from Harstad. I thanked the crew members who had come to my rescue –

Roy, the steward, and the waitress and inserted my next film. Roy said that he'd ring the club in Hammerfest about replacing my membership card. It was fortunate that the crewman Karl had introduced me to Roy earlier.

The island of Andoya ahead looked like a giant aircraft carrier with a low central section and a fairly mountainous superstructure fore and aft. We didn't head directly for it but performed a slight curve leftwards in an obviously strictly delineated channel with close markers for a kilometre or so. Even in daylight, this was useful – crucial in the dark, I should imagine. The actual navigable channel was quite narrow, and the bottom with all its detail could easily be seen on either side of the *Lofoten*. One could actually see the very shallow waters deepen as the underwater precipices opened up to reveal the chasm which we must follow. I could watch this feature better from the stern of the boat. My friend, the 'Oslo Geordie', said that it had to be continuously dredged to remain navigable.

We arrived for a stop at Risøyhamn at the south end of the island of Andoya. On walking to the nearby concrete bridge I found good vantage points for photos. One was of the snowy mountain peaks on the island on our side of the bridge, whilst another was a view of the pre-dawn sun reflecting off the sound separating us from the mainland. That bridge linked Andoya and its fishing stocks with the mainland markets.

My 'Oslo Geordie' friend and I had another chat. His knowledge of boats and shipping was extensive and interesting. Various markings on the hull were explained to me including the important 18′ line which was very relevant in the context of the recent narrow channel.

Although the sun had earlier risen to 6° to 7° above the

horizon, it still set at 11.20 hrs as it slowly descended behind the mountains. I had the suspicion that the photographs that I'd taken at midday would be underexposed. Was I right? Only time would tell.

I had a longer chat with the lady with whom I'd spoken that morning and we compared experiences. She was there as part of her job which was in northern Holland where she represented a Travel Company. She and her friend were looking for hotels and would eventually disembark at Bodø.

I had a short walk on my own at Risøyhamn, lonely without my Dutch friends who were exploring the boat as part of their job. Back aboard, I watched the scenery all the way south to Sortland. It was there where I joined my two Dutch friends and went for a walk heading from the harbour towards town. Noting the time of day and the distance to the town from the harbour, I planned to walk seven minutes each way before the boat's departure. We chatted away amicably and profusely in English on the way to town. I looked anxiously at my watch as the time neared seven minutes, but the girls showed no concern at all. At a street market, they were engrossed in clothing and other items while I, because of my worries about the time which I hadn't mentioned to them, indicated my interest in another stall and then a return to the boat.

Once I 'hit' the road, somewhat behind plan, my legs moved like greased lightning, intermittently jogging and running to avoid missing the boat. I wondered whether the girls had some other unspoken plans for their stay, but, looking back I could see no signs of them at all.

At the first glimpse of the boat, it was still there, thank goodness. I realized that I was late for the planned departure time, and as I rounded a building on the harbour, I could see the crew taking up the gang plank. My heart rate immediately trebled from its already semi-panic rate as I gesticulated and called to them. As I neared the vessel its engines were being throttled up in power for take-off. The friendly crew quickly throttled back and waved to me. This was the *basic* ship-to-shore communications! As I arrived alongside the boat they indicated that I could jump but I was reluctant to make this life-threatening move. I realized that they were joking and then they, again, relowered the gangplank! All the time, I was thanking them very profusely in an exhausted state, whilst telling them that I was *not* the only one left there – 'there are two Dutch ladies in town!' They discussed this in Norwegian, and the boat, with me on board but the girls still ashore, took off slowly southwards, hugging the coast of the island of Langoy.

I still kept trying unsuccessfully to spot my friends somewhere ashore, but eventually we slowed up at an unscheduled quay and there, thank goodness, I could see them arriving in a fast car! As we got closer I could see they were still as jovial as ever, but half-hiding their faces, still smiling but partly in embarrassment and in shame. 'We feel so embarrassed and such fools' was one of the comments they uttered as the ship slowed down. So Dutch people, when communicating with Norwegians, still use English – unless those two ladies wanted *me* to understand.

They re-embarked safely and cheerfully. Even the crew was cheerful – but they always were! We welcomed them back on board and they explained to me and the crew what had happened. They knew what time they had to return to the boat but, unfortunately, their new watch was telling the wrong time. They had estimated about an hour for the stop, whereas my calculation had earlier shown that twenty minutes was the correct planned stopping time. No wonder they showed no concern when I *was* feeling concerned.

They didn't have any contingency plans but had indeed been very concerned when they realized they had been abandoned on a remote offshore Norwegian island with little money and no documentation. They told me later that if they hadn't rejoined the boat where they did, they would have hired a taxi to the next scheduled quay at Stokmarkness. Things happened so quickly after such a leisurely walk!

By mealtime they had clearly recovered and we chatted sociably about their feelings and thoughts from our adjacent tables. At Stokmarkness, obviously not fully recovered, the girls decided to stay aboard. I bade them a brief farewell and walked to the nice little town where they were building a bypass from the end of the shopping centre. Was it there that I had seen a cinema advertizing its showing of *Jurassic Park* that week? I managed to get a little bit of shopping done before returning to the boat, where I carried on talking with Reitje and Pascale. Reitje offered the name Maria as an easier alternative for my English tongue before the girls went off on an 'official tour' of the cabins – just the job! Maria, which was her second name, promised to send me a photograph of the Northern Lights which she had taken, if I gave her my address. I made it out when next in my cabin and Maria seemed well pleased when I gave it to her.

As the *Lofoten* headed out of the Trollfjord, half an hour from Svolvaer, it *hit* the open sea because these islands are quite a way from the coast of the mainland. Unusually, I had managed to adapt to the waves by then but the two girls were sitting it out, in the foyer/lounge outside the restaurant. We chatted for a while until the increasing choppiness of the sea clearly affected their stomachs. They then went for a lie-down in their cabin as they wanted to be fit in time for their research into hotels in Svolvaer.

I further explored the boat whilst on its choppy way south but part of the time I relaxed in my cabin, my home in this bobbing ping-pong ball. Eventually the PA system announced that we were just arriving, half an hour ahead of schedule. We would thus arrive at 17.45 hrs and depart at 19.15 hrs, the board near the top of the gangplank reminding us of this fact. I went out onto the quay to see the town whilst the girls did their research and fact-finding in hotels. My excursion was in two phases, with a return to the cabin for writing notes between them. First, whilst the girls headed off to some likely hotels, I headed for the centre of Svolvaer. On my second outing I bought some postcards, including some with polar bears and some others with different views of the Northern Lights.

Pascale told me that they had found two hotels. She was the 'writer' whilst Reitje was the photographer. I really looked forward to seeing Reitje's photos later in the year, but was apprehensive of what could be achieved even though she had a much better camera than mine and was a professional.

After the evening meal, I bade a fond farewell to my new-found friends as they had decided to return to the beds in their cabin – for the sea was becoming very 'uncomfortable'! I survived this worst ever sea crossing in my life – although not with the worst effects – because I was getting used to it with my newly found countermeasures. My latest techniques for avoiding sea sickness were put into practice (see Annex C). Thus I layed flat on my back and stayed in that position no matter what the boat did, my eyes closed and with a sweet to suck within easy range so as not to shift the position of my body whilst trying to retrieve it. By using this technique I survived that leg of the journey, although we still hadn't done the crossing to the mainland. We arrived at Stamsund half an hour late so would be departing late. What a surprise!

I couldn't find Pascale or 'Maria' but guessed that they were trying to recover. The Hurtigrute left at 22.00 hrs on the start of a very rough crossing. I used the same technique for preventing sea sickness whilst awake, including putting sweets in my pockets to minimize body movement during 'retrieval time'.

I awoke and got dressed at 02.10 hrs as I particularly wanted to say goodbye to my two Dutch friends. I met them near the gangplank descent to Bodø and we all kissed farewell and gave each other good wishes for the future. Once down the gangplank, Rietje and Pascale got into the waiting taxi and disappeared into the town. A lonely feeling overtook me at their departure so I returned to my cabin and got some more sleep. It was now Saturday, 13 November and the last twenty-four hours had certainly been eventful!

Chapter XI

Return to Trondheim

With a tyre screech as if from a gangster movie, the boat skidded to a halt at Ørnes harbour. This was the last stop before leaving the Arctic Circle and I woke at 07.37 hrs to find it pitch dark. I had photographed the place on the outward trip including, for example, the Willemsen's shop! 'Williamson' was my ex-wife's maiden name.

I got dressed ready for the next place after breakfast, but even more important, to take photos of the Arctic Circle's crossing-point before then. On the breakfast table was a letter from Reitje and Pascale which they had obviously left for me a few hours earlier. I got Roy at *Resepsjon* to stamp my 'Circle' and 'Nordkapp' cards with the appropriate dates for both directions. He was only too willing to oblige.

At 09.51 hrs, we passed the island with the globe marking the Arctic Circle and I took three photos from different angles. The horn blew a second or two before the final photo so I knew we were now back in civilization – or had we just *left* civilization?

We made slow progress but with excellent visibility from the 'Circle' to Nesna. No bus could keep to a timetable if the road was moving at half speed in the opposite direction! That day, furthermore, the wind speed was three to five times our speed through the water, but again in the opposite direction. Fortunately this leg of the journey was relatively smooth after the overnight sea-crossing.

At Nesna, there was only time for a four-minute stop, a single photo of a yellowish house and a few hurried words with a woman walking her dog. That was a *cargo only* stop, the main business of our craft.

Even before Nesna, the dazzling sun was at the incredibly high elevation, now, of 5° making the use of sunglasses almost obligatory! Despite its elevation that day, it still set before midday, but this time it was due to obscuration by mountains.

Never mind! It will rise again! Oh, yes – it will rise again.

It did too!!

Sandnessjøen was an interesting place. I did a bit of sightseeing there and took some photos including some of 'Car-Eating-Boats' with their mouths open wide to swallow whole cars and lorries before they scurried off along the coast somewhere. In addition to our own long-distance craft (i.e. to North Pole and back) there were local ferries to Dønna and elsewhere. There was even one boat called *North Crusader* and labelled with RESCUE ZONE in giant capital letters. I heard from the locals that it supplied the North Sea oil industry.

I took photos after leaving the port, including one of Sandnessjøen and another of the Seven Sisters. The best view of those mountains was whilst I was in my cabin, all nice and snug. The only problem with that potentially excellent photo was that the 'beast' decided automatically to take it as a 'flash' so that a bright white reflection from the window resulted. Moving south, we drifted past the 'Sisters', exposing themselves one by one! By way of explanation, the 'Sisters' are, visually, a set of mountains separated by valleys caused by immense glacial action which cut a single mountain into separate peaks and deep valleys running down towards the sea.

On the way further south, I could see an airstrip's VOR system, just north of Alstahaug at Stokka. Quite a lot of interesting equipment there! For lunch we had fried herrings as described by the Chief Steward some time before and I asked the waitress about the possibility, being a radar man, of going onto the ship's bridge. She made enquiries and came back with the answer that I could 'go straight up after lunch', if I liked. 'You're welcome,' she added, and asked me if I wanted coffee here in the restaurant or on the bridge. I chose the latter option and thanked her very much.

A few minutes after lunch, I went up. Annex D contains a summary of my findings and the answers to the questions that I asked. Some replies were direct, but others I had to deduce when the question was not understood. Because the boat's pilot was not familiar with the English version of some of the technical terms, some detail could not be explored but that was my fault for my lack of a Norwegian vocabulary. Apart from that, the pilot spoke very good English.

At Bronnøysund, I went ashore for a couple of walks. On the first, it proved to be a bit damp so I returned for my parka for a more extensive exploration. Blast-off from the launch pad was at 17.00 hrs. It was foggy on deck, so I went inside to the enclosed areas of decks and foyers and encountered a large crowd of disabled (spastic) people on board for a trip. It was easier to understand them than the 'fluent' Norwegians because I found that their 'speaking' was very similar to that back in the UK, and so communication was partially visual and partially verbal.

There was some 'easy-listening' music *live* on an accordion in the lounge by the dining room, probably for the disabled, as there hadn't been any *live* music since take-off from Bergen many days before. It was very crowded there and the music was great. This was followed by a sumptuous dinner – as usual. The staff kept coming up with winners every time!

On arrival at Rørvik halfway along the waterway, I indulged myself in a very pleasant walk. On our way north, I'd been unable to do so as it had been dark and I was awaiting my first view of the Aurora Borealis. This time I was able to see the attractiveness of this little town, which gave one the experience of being, in parts, like a slightly large 'Legoland'. Very delightful!

Waiting close to the *Lofoten* was the M/S *Midnatsol*, one of our sister ships, on which the handicapped party would return northwards on their short trip. They were continuously running excitedly up and down the very long and steep gangplank before they finally went aboard. Their excitement was very plain for all to see.

On meeting crewman Roy, he told me that my Membership Card of the Ice Bear Club would be sent to Malvern as the girl at the club remembered my joining. He also said that the two young girls on board were part of a Youth Training Scheme and he answered my question about 'fridge magnets' as I was attempting to buy some for my sister-in-law. He said that he'd never seen any in Norway.

Back on board, I had a look around the *Dusjrom* which turned out to be a shower room, somewhat spacious compared to Pascale's description of their size on the more modern ships. She had said that essentially the modern ones (or at least the ladies' ones) required the user to sit on a small toilet-like seat whilst being sprayed from above. The 'room' on those must obviously be somewhat smaller than on the *Lofoten*.

The Rørvik bridge-clearance seemed to be a few more inches than on our way north, but still mind-bogglingly small! The Aurora was visible until the clouds ruined it! At dinner, the handicapped people and their helpers occupied seven tables each of six people. Each had a personal helper. Sometimes, the helper had to act as a restrainer because some of them had quite boisterous personalities and were full of life.

The long overnight voyage to Trondheim was enjoyable despite waking several times but, by now, I had used 'mind-over-matter' and other techniques to overcome seasickness. We docked at 06.35 hrs on 14 November and, for a change, I made use of my battery shaver. I had an early ten-minute stroll just before the 08.00 hrs breakfast. We were at a different dock from the one we used on the way up the coast and, furthermore, it was much colder now, with extremely thick frost on the roads and pavements – just eight days since I had been there last!!

I followed my usual practice of taking a different route to my previous visit in order to obtain a more varied overall picture of the place that I was revisiting. Each revisit to a town is *not* entirely different, but certain common elements to enable the whole picture to be correlated. To enable me to do this, I took with me my Malvern library book *Insights Guide – Norway* which had a useful map of Trondheim.

Rather than go to Nidaros Cathedral and the Castle, I crossed the River Nidelva at its first bridge, a rail bridge with footpath and a small road section also. I thus went over the Nedre Elvehvn to a little-used part of Trondheim, and then took a footpath to regain the unnamed road system, eventually joining the named sections at Innhervedsvei and back over the river by the Bakkebiu. I then crossed the Kjopmannsgata and went into the reasonably attractive shopping areas of Tryggvasonsgata and Søndregt. After going across the Østiekanal-haven which was a sort of harbour/canal, I rejoined first the railway lines at Hovedstusjon, and secondly, my old route back to the docks about a kilometre away.

On leaving Trondheim, I again followed the map that the Captain had given me on my first day so that I could relate the sightings with the names on it. We slowly proceeded down the Trondheimfjord making the long right-hand bend to head for the Norwegian Sea with, on our right, the same places that we had passed on 6 November. This is a tranquil coast. There was Lady Austrat's castle, where that powerful lady entertained her influential guests. After the straight leg following the right-hand bend in the fjord, we turned left to get closer to the Sea, passing the NATO base of Ørland on our right as before. However, instead of going right around this promontory and heading north as before, we carried on southwards this time, the main coast on our left with the islands of Hitra and Smøla passing to the right. It was so relaxing seeing these beautiful sights glide past at a snail's pace, or 15 knots in reality. Apart from the boxes of fish and other freight taken by our vessel, there was now a goat in a cage outside one window!

It was clearly different further south (at 64° North) as at 13.20 hrs, not only had the sun not set, but it was still at the incredible altitude of 12°. We had left Trondheim at 10.00 hrs and, on settling in to my private table in the restaurant, I indulged myself in another marvellous meal. This one had the most fantastic mutton that I'd ever tasted, and the potatoes were roasted in butter after being boiled in something special. Many other lovely vegetables accompanied this main course and, for sweet, the artistry of the ice cream made one feel guilty about eating it.

As we passed the island of Smøla, I spent a fair chunk of the afternoon watching an almost infinite string of islands drift past to our right, starting before Smøla and emanating from the southern tip of Hitra. They were all very small but extended well over ten miles, taking us right into Kristiansund. At one time, with the curious optical effects with the refraction at low angles over the sea, they all seemed to be joined up. They were not, of course, but it was a battle between the eyes and the brain to come to that conclusion.

I had a late-afternoon walk around Kristiansund's front near the harbour. It was a delightful place and had an attractive approach. It was a pity that we were not there longer for it had been dark on our way northwards too! It had a nice shopping area on the front which I did not use however. The spare 'town map' that I got from *Resepsjon* proved invaluable.

Later, I indulged in some relaxation in my cabin on the bed before the sea-crossing to Molde further south. There was a fantastic 'fish-preparation' for an evening meal. I thought the cheeseboard was French, but it had Norwegian Camembert and Norwegian Blue Vein encased in pure white-bread sandwiches. Great!

Later, at about 21.00 hrs, I walked part of the way into the centre of Molde, but there was not enough time allowed. It was far too big a place to explore, but the approach by night made the town look attractive with its many lights.

As expected, the night leg proved very rough and I first awoke at 01.15 hrs with the boat already at Alesund. I had enjoyed Alesund going northwards – a memorable meander around the town and surrounding hills – but, alas, the time of night prevented me from revisiting it. Awake now, I realized that it was rough sooner than expected. I shut my eyes for a few seconds and entered a time warp, opening them again at 02.10 hrs, thereby luckily missing the heavy open seas of the Stad. Unfortunately, I had missed Torvik – but we were behind time now in very heavy seas. I had the impression that the autopilot had been set incorrectly and that we were heading something like north-west towards Iceland, across the Norwegian Sea, with the helmsman asleep somewhere in his cabin.

Who needed poltergeists when loose objects in my own and adjacent cabins kept falling and noisily rolling around the floor by natural causes? I had to get up and risk the possibility of seasickness in order to recover and secure items in *my* cabin at least. It became abundantly obvious now, if it wasn't earlier, why tables, chairs and other furniture were chained to the floor. I had thought, during my first hour or so on board the *Lofoten*, that they had a problem with theft. Not so! It was these poltergeists that they had to guard against. Anyway, I made several trips about the cabin, only mind-over-matter preventing me from being seasick. Only just!

It was possible to get a little rest at Maløy after the torture of the last leg from Torvik around the Stad. After Maløy, came some on-and-off sleep until a rude awakening as we shuddered to a stop at Florø. We sneaked quietly out whilst

I was writing my notes after the dressing and toilet activities. So we were now on the final leg of the return to Bergen, not having stood on solid ground since Kristiansund late in the afternoon of the day before.

For breakfast, I had some Lett Melk on my cereals, followed by cheese, meat and biscuits, with a glass of H-Mjolk. A choice of milks always appeared, but on that occasion I did not use any Culture Melk! During breakfast, the sea became relatively calm (now 15 November). Individual wave-heights were less than a foot, which was tolerable. However, the swell was much worse at four feet in amplitude but with a lower (queasy) frequency. This low frequency was 'tuned' to the *Lofoten*'s natural pitching frequency for our current speed – and thus our pitching motion was amplified. When side-on to this swell, it produced some alarming roll amplitudes.

I took an internal cabin photo for trip memories during this period before we got too near Bergen, and used most of the morning for rest, relaxation and recovery. I strolled along to the restaurant somewhat earlier than normal for lunch at 12.10 hrs to find that I was the only one there! Perhaps everyone else was either still recovering or packing in readiness for our arrival at Bergen.

For lunch, I started with a delightful 'Eggs in Mushroom Soup', following that with 'Fried Halibut' with a number of sauces. I still prefer the tartare sauce taste to the Salad Cream provided with this dish! For sweet, the cherries and various sauces satisfied my taste buds. The Chief Steward paid me a personal visit during the meal, bade me farewell and gave me an invitation to 'come and see us anytime'. I told him that I'd love to – and that I'd be writing and talking about the voyage in some detail back in the UK.

The crew member, Roy, who was normally in reception, also came to bid me a personal farewell, and I received a public farewell over the loudspeakers around the craft.

As we prepared to disembark, datalink and other communications to and from the *Lofoten* were very busy. Teletypes were busy with the details on the requirements for taxis – and so on. The Hurtigrute, although an old 'traditional' craft, had modern electronics, satellite navigation equipment and communications to aid it in the modern world.

Chapter XII

Arrival in Olde Bryggen

We eventually docked in Bergen harbour and my personal transport picked me up and took me to the old part of town, Bryggen, to a new type of hotel, the Orion Bryggen. It was very nice, but the best part about it was in its location in a harbour setting! I also had a 'non-smoking' room, unpolluted by any previous occupant.

After sorting myself out by early afternoon, I went for a leisurely walk around Olde Bryggen, its harbour, its fish market and its medieval warehouses. These were still in use, attractive, well-preserved and recognized as one of the world's great treasures. It still felt as though it was a genuine part of the Hanseatic traders' empire.

Between walks in the pouring rain, for Bergen is like that folks, the TV in my hotel room had some 'Euro Sport' on satellite and other channels. These revealed a broad range of programmes including tennis, speed yachting, windsurfing, and even more important for me, personally, was the appearance of a friend who I had not seen for a year or more – namely Ian Sweet, an expert and commentator on the World Triathlon Championships in Turkey. He had been a computer expert in the RAF, working at the same place as me.

Ian had always excelled in his professional approach to Sports Management which he intended to do full-time after his demob from the RAF. Even then he was very active in finding sponsors for triathletes.

The next morning I had breakfast at 07.30 hrs after decoding the lift buttons labelled OPP and NED. Pity I don't speak Norwegian, isn't it? For the first time on this adventure, it was an 'English-style' breakfast with a variety of the inevitable fried items. So one cannot eat healthily ALL the time out here! However, it was not all bad because the ingredients were prepared in the Norwegian way. Whilst eating and not being able to communicate with many people because of my lack of Scandinavian languages, I soon got the impression in this International hotel that the majority of the guests were business people. The hotel had a great taste in music for breakfast over the discretely-volumed loudspeakers – country music, I love it! Naturally, here it was mostly with, I guess, Norwegian lyrics but the *feeling* was still there. However, they still had some of the Canadian Anne Murray with a beautiful backing on electric-pedal-steel guitar, and a welcome appearance by the Everley Brothers singing real Country as well – what more could one ask for? Good ol' Don and Phil!

Back in my room, there was a Scandinavian version of 'Come Dancing' on the Euro Sport channel – and it was Latin-American time!

It was time to look around Bryggen. Through the automatic doors – with their overactive imaginations. I got 'lost', in the nicest possible way, in the medieval wooden buildings, workshops, trading offices, craft shops and professional premises – it was just fantastic. With it being so old, it made me grieve over what the planners and builders had done to our own local Tewkesbury. Tewkesbury *could* have been like this, I was sure, but yuppy developments had changed the 'Olde English' character of the place. Bryggen hadn't fallen into that same trap – and the world is grateful for it. It is a major 'listing' with UNESCO!

There was a funicular railway further up the hill above the town, but who needed a funicular when there was such an attractive area to browse around on foot? Given another day or two, the funicular might have been added to my 'visits list' there.

Bryggen, including the medieval wooden wharf complex, was a three-dimensional maze, one of the world's best, if not the best, for history and culture in a medieval settlement. More than just an older version of Tewkesbury, it has hills behind, which more than matched the charm of Malvern and its hills. It had steep slopes, paths and roads in town which provided one with attractive walks. Housing was tightly packed, so at any point, one could stop, regain one's breath, look at the amazing variety of houses, most of which were wooden, wallow in the tremendous views of the harbour, the olde town, the hills – and any combination of these that you so desire. The higher reaches of this part of town reminded me of mountain villages in the south of France overlooking the Mediterranean, places such as Bormes and Ézé. Furthermore, there was a likeness to Hawkeshead in the English Lake District, but without the dreaded extensive commercialization. Olde Bergen was still very much a 'lived-in' town rather than a tourist showpiece.

If this trip hadn't taken me to the fjords, arctic scenery, snow and ice, and the Aurora, I would want to remember Norway purely for this fantastic place. Bryggen, you're terrific! For your angled cobblestones, your everything! And bearing in mind that my entire stay in Bergen was in the pouring rain, I still felt a love for the place. It would have been even more fantastic had it been in dry weather! Still, we *were* on the fringe of the Arctic in winter!

Back in my room at the Orion, I heard some Country Music from the next room. It was a selection by the 'Cleaners' on some (TV?) channel at 10.15 hrs. I quickly found it in my own room on channel No 1. It had Norma Jean's rendition of 'Candle in the wind' plus other singers and songs. That morning I felt awkward in the hotel, where I had difficulty balancing and coping with a non-moving deck. Still, after eleven days and 2,500 miles travelling around a choppy coastline, it was to be expected. However, I overcame it comparatively quickly.

That morning's TV gave me more of Ian Sweet's presentations on the World Triathlon Championships at Alanya in Turkey. After a bit more sporting TV, I got my own legs working again for walks around and about Bryggen, a delightful place which has all of Malvern, ancient Tewkesbury, the better parts of Hawkeshead, San Francisco, Ézé and Bormes included in its wonders. It also has piss-istent, non-stop rain which had been continuous from my early awakening until my departure.

Before being taken to the airport, I waited in the hotel foyer talking with some Norwegians and Germans, having had to vacate my room by midday. It was a good job they all spoke English! Eventually, my transport arrived, and again I was the sole passenger, this time to the Airport. We left ten minutes later than I had previously scheduled. However our delay had been radio-phoned to the hotel and I finally left at 15.35 hrs. The same driver collected me as when I arrived. Now I was off to Friesland (Bergen) airport in a very comfortable minibus with eight passenger seats, plus driver, complete with two electronic voice links and a data link with printouts.

Due to the delay we headed off at high speed despite the heavy rain but we were not on 'slicks'. He had opted for wet-weather tyres for this race! I think most competitors had made the same choice! Our tyre choice held us well in a four-wheel drift that we made on a bend in an underpass. I wondered how the wet got there! There were other underpasses for our amusement – but longer and straighter. We eventually arrived at Friesland where I checked in and answered some odd questions because I kept on activating their bleeper! On inspection by curious airport staff, the object of interest proved not to be the camera, as I had supposed, but one of the shavers. I'd never seen it by X-Ray vision before. But now I knew how it worked!

Following this, I made my way along to Gate 23 for flight SK517, having specified a seat in a non-smoking area. Bergen airport's tax-free area was relatively quiet but it was 'all go' on my way through twelve days earlier. A digital display showed me that the ETD, the estimated time of departure, for SK517 was 17.35 hrs so I had a little while to spare with some Kroners to spend and some American girls to talk to. I tried to convince them that the duty-free prices were higher than in *ordinary* shops in England which was where they were going next.

A delayed departure was expected because of the plane's late arrival from Copenhagen. Now I could see it through my binoculars. As it arrived at the terminal building I could make out its name. It was the 'Margret Viking'.

Using the Norwegian taps at the airport revived memories of the various hotel rooms with their unusual taps, although I had got used to them as they appeared to be a Norwegian standard tap, very user-friendly, very effective. It is a mixer-tap which controlled both the flow-rate (up/down movement) and temperature (left/right movement), so one could fly it like an aircraft with a joystick! One could move in two planes simultaneously, for example, when wanting to decrease the flow-rate AND temperature, one moved the single control mechanism downwards and to the left. I grew to love this system.

Chapter XIII

I Ride Margret to London

On arrival at seat 20A (a non-smoker) I settled in comfortably to enjoy the 'Margret Viking's' amenities. As we taxied out towards the runway it became clear that an inch or so layer of snow covered the grass of the airport. Our pilot used his de-icer spray to de-ice the wings but more importantly to prevent their icing up in flight. I am sure that this was achieved by an easier method than in a car. I'd not taken off in snow before, but it was too late to back out now, even if I'd wanted to!

This MD87 aircraft was of the same family as the one that brought me to Bergen via Stavanger. Whilst on the launch pad, it revved up its engines to full power with rattling and shaking movements threatening to blow the plane apart. Then we surged along the runway with considerable acceleration and after a 23-second run, reached take-off speed at 17.51 hrs. Goodbye Bergen! I needed to put my watch back an hour now, but being *digital* it required an advance of twenty-three hours!

The MD87 is a 110-seater with a maximum take-off weight of 61 tons, is 39.8 metres long with a wingspan of 33 metres and will cruise at 505 m.p.h. guzzling 3,600 litres an hour of our precious fuel for its JT8D-217C Pratt & Whitney engines. For our high-powered takeoff run, it would have been drinking much faster than that!

When up to a reasonable altitude, our meals arrived. I

had a cold, yellow fish with salad items including asparagus. A roll accompanied the meal, as did an orange drink, a lovely dessert and coffee afterwards. The coffee was different with a beautiful taste and presentation befitting the Norwegians.

I accepted a newspaper, *The Independent*, and settled down for a pleasant flight. It was, of course, too dark to see any scenery, so the newspaper was welcome. In lighter conditions, I still always prefer to see as much of the scenery as possible whatever the altitude.

Our approach to Heathrow was uneventful for us passengers, but the pilot's use of the throttle indicated multiple alterations probably dealing with changes in both cross-track and along-track winds, together with variations in angle-of-attack, and anything else that might have been necessary. Touchdown was at 6.38 p.m. (London time) and the pilot also 'played' with his throttle on the ground during the taxying phase to Terminal 3. We had to queue, with about a dozen aircraft, to wait our turn to cross a taxiway. Multiple decelerations, as well as accelerations to high speed, made me think that the pilot was doing a 'lap of honour' at racing speed! During this complementary tour of the Heathrow tarmac and, for all I know, the whole of the west side of London, I spotted a Concorde doing an even higher-speed pass in the opposite direction but parallel to our course. I believe it must have been either taking off or landing – but it wasn't in view long enough to establish which!

We arrived at the aircraft park, and accelerated yet again so that by the time we'd finished 'playing about' it was eleven minutes after touchdown before we came to a stop. I undid my seatbelt at 19.17 hours, disembarked, recovered my luggage and made my way with others to the Underground system that links the airport with Central London.

My arrival at the Tregaron Hotel – I'll actually be in the Ashley Hotel part – was at 20.20 hours. Here, in Norfolk Square, three formerly independently-owned hotels had been joined together into one. The breakfast area for the three was in the basement of the Oasis Hotel.

Because of the weight of all my luggage, I made two trips up the many floors to my room. It was certainly easier than the 'single trip' that I had made whilst on the way to Norway earlier in the month! I turned the oppressive central heating off between the loads. The place was always overheated. At last in my own room, settled, I lapped up a TV comedy, some news broadcasts and a discussion programme. For a break from TV, I visited a Hole-in-the-Wall machine near Paddington Station, just a walk around the corner – these machines being called Mini-Banks in Norway. This Paddington Mini-Bank didn't give me a statement after the transaction, but an electronic message prior to the request *did* warn me. Whilst out, I called at my 'usual' fish and chip shop and took my purchase back to the hotel room to eat in comfort and in a quieter environment than this same hotel in Norfolk Square had provided on my way out on 3 November.

The next day started for me at 7 a.m. on 17 November when I got up and ready for the last leg of the journey home. There was no en-suite facility here in England at this hotel, so it's an 'upstairs and downstairs' expedition. I opened the curtains at 7.22 a.m. before breakfast, the view already revealing a cloudy, dismal day – but much brighter than midday was at North Cape about a week earlier. Radio 2 broadcast some hazardous *icy road* warnings, the sort of everyday driving conditions for motoring in Norway!

At breakfast time, I chose the opposite side of the table

that I'd had earlier in the month for the express purpose of not having to look at the steam and heat each time someone emerged from the kitchen. I was three rows from this 'inferno', but unfortunately the temperature still burned my back!

Paying my bill at reception, I was told that it was 'cold and icy outside' to which I commented 'Thank goodness', and then explained my remark in terms of the Arctic visit that I'd just completed. It certainly looked warm enough outside from my 3rd floor window, and it proved to be so when I got outside as well. I was clad only in an open-necked shirt, because case-carrying would soon have me sweltering. I was more then warm enough, too hot in fact, although if I hadn't been carrying cases it would have been cool and pleasant enough for the few minutes' walk to Paddington mainline station.

As if under computer control, the train accelerated out of Paddington, being not as smooth, laterally, as an aircraft. This motion made it impossible to write despite the longitudinal smoothness. Just before Oxford, the digital notice in the carriage now changed its mind about the train, altering it from 'Thames Express' to 'Cotswold Express'. New sequences of messages then appeared on its display.

Arrival at Malvern Link Station was 11.24 a.m., my taxi getting me home at 11.31 a.m. I then did the 'appliance of science' and launched the Zanussi automatic washing machine at 11.39 a.m. on its first mission after my arrival. That must have given it a shock, less then eight minutes after stepping inside the door! I realize that I'm home and the expedition is over – the next one will be to Iceland in June/July 1994. I can't wait!

Annex A
The Schedule – My Expedition through the Arctic Circle

Day No.	Date	Itinerary	Night at
1	3/11/93	Malvern to Paddington (Rail) (1.49 p.m.–4.16 p.m.)	Tregaron Hotel Paddington (4.40ish)
2	4/11/93	Underground to Heathrow (8.30–9.30) Heathrow to Bergen, Norway. (Flight SK516) (10.40–14.30) (via Stavanger) Free Transfer from airport to coastal boat Boat departs 22.00 hrs	Cabin 305 (Type D1 outside) in *Lofoten*
3	5/11/93	Florø, Maløy, Tørvik, **Alesund**, Molde, Kristiansund	Cabin 305 *Lofoten*
4	6/11/93	**TRONDHEIM**, Rørvik	Cabin 305 *Lofoten*

Day No.	Date	Itinerary	Night at
5	7/11/93	Bronnoysund, Sandnessjoen, Nesna, ENTER ARCTIC CIRCLE, Ørnes, **Bodø**, Stamsund, **Svolvaer**	Cabin 305 *Lofoten*
6	8/11/93	Stokmarknes, Sortland, Risøyhamn, **Harstad**, Finnsnes, **TROMSØ**, Skjervoy	Cabin 305 *Lofoten*
7	9/11/93	Oksfjord, **Hammerfest**, Havoysund, **Honningsvag**, Kjollefjord, Mehamn, Berlevag	Cabin 305 *Lofoten*
8	10/11/93	Batsfjord, Vardo, **Kirkenes**, Vadso, Vardo, Batsfjord, Berlevag	Cabin 305 *Lofoten*
9	11/11/93	Mehamn, Kjollefjord, Honningsvag, Havoysund, **Hammerfest**, Oksfjord, Skjervoy	Cabin 305 *Lofoten*
10	12/11/93	**Tromsø**, Finnsnes, **Harstad**, Risøyhamn, Sortland, Stokmarknes, **Svolvaer**, Stamsund	Cabin 305 *Lofoten*

Day No.	Date	Itinerary	Night at
11	13/11/93	**BODØ**, Ørnes, LEAVE ARCTIC CIRCLE, Nesna, Sandnessjoen, Bronnoysund, Rorvik	Cabin 305, *Lofoten*
12	14/11/93	**TRONDHEIM**, Kristiansund, Molde, **Alesund**	Cabin 305 *Lofoten*
13	15/11/93	Torvik, Maloy, Florø, **BERGEN**, (Arrive 14.00 hrs) Free Transfer to Hotel	Bryggen Orion Hotel (Bergen)
14	16/11/93	Free Transfer – Hotel to Airport Bergen to Heathrow (Flight SK517) (17.25–18.30 hrs) Underground to Paddington (7.0–8.0 p.m.)	Tregaron Hotel Paddington
15	17/11/93	Rail to Malvern (8.48–11.24 a.m.)	Home

Key to stops made by the Hurtegruten (Coastal Boats):

General (Half-hour)	Shown in ordinary print
Longer (Over 2 hrs)	Shown in **Bold** print
Major (3½–6 hrs)	Shown in **BOLD CAPITALS**

The World's most northerly city (Hammerfest) is way north of Alaska's most northerly town (Barrow) and was visited on 9 and 11 November. On those same days, the closest approach to the North Pole was made, near Mehamn.

Annex B
The Arctic Circle

Why is the Arctic Circle, in common with the Antarctic, different from other places on the Earth's surface?

To answer that, one must recognize that the Earth is tilted on its axis from the plane of its orbit around the Sun. That tilt is about 23.5° which is why the northern hemisphere is warmer than the southern hemisphere from March to September each year, and why it is colder in other months.

Consider the diagram on page 100, with the Earth's inclination to its orbit exaggerated. The vertical line is perpendicular to the plane of the orbit, the directions to the sun in mid-winter and mid-summer being as indicated.

The axis of the Earth is the one on which it spins. This, basically, is always the same direction in space. Thus, in summer, the right-hand side is illuminated and for a point on the globe rotating once each twenty-four hours approximately, the length of the 'day' (i.e. daylight) is longer than for a point on the northern half than for a point on the southern half. A very simple piece of imagination shows that for points north of the Arctic Circle in mid-summer there is no darkness during the day as the sun *does not set.*

In summertime, similarly, imagine a point inside the Antarctic Circle throughout the day which is mid-summer

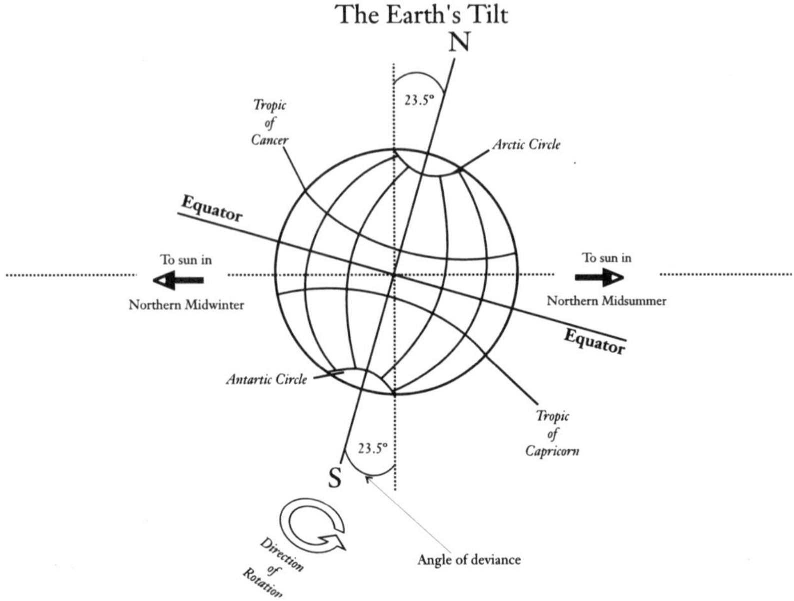

in the northern hemisphere. The sun *never rises* on that day. The same happens in the northern hemisphere in our mid-winter – the sun never rises anywhere in the Arctic Circle. In fact for the North and South Poles the year consists of only one day and one night that last six months each. The 'Arctic Night's' duration depends on latitude, being from six months long at the pole to non-existent outside the Arctic Circle. For North Cape, the Arctic Night starts at the beginning of December, with the sun making its next appearance in February! You will see that I left the area just before the Arctic Night started, but the days were very short, with a midday sun only a degree above the horizon! In fact, the 'Land of the Midnight Sun' became 'The Land of the Midday Night'.

This makes photography very challenging to impossible.

Specialist films and cameras are really required. My automatic one, cheap and cheerful, was not really appropriate, but my trip was for personal experiences and feelings that do not lend themselves readily to the camera. Thus, my decision, once on the way, was to put those experiences and feelings into words rather than on film – hence this book!

The Norwegian coast, although largely within the 'Circle', isn't all *that* cold even in the winter. That's my personal view but others may differ. Certainly, it gets colder the further north one gets, but this is moderated by the warmth of the Gulf Stream when the wind is from the west. In fact, I frequently found it quite comfortable when standing, without a jacket, on the open decks, even within the 'circle'. When the sun was shining from the vast elevation of 5° above the horizon, I was sometimes able to go out with a sleeveless shirt and no jacket.

It is a different matter altogether when the wind is blowing from the east across the Kola peninsular or when one is on land! I witnessed this in Hammerfest (see p. 45) on 9 November (see p. 96). Without a thermometer it was impossible to estimate those temperatures which were beyond all my previous experiences. On changing out of an ordinary jacket and into the essential parka, it then became very comfortable indeed.

Annex C
Conquering Seasickness

Early in the 2,500 miles of the *Lofoten*'s travels by fjords and open seas, the difference between the two sorts of water was like chalk and cheese. The former type was like a calm ride on a nice boat on a millpond; the latter was like a torture chamber where sickness was always waiting to happen!

Due to my stomach's history, seasickness was never very far away and I could not avoid it – even on the Isle of Wight ferry! So, maybe, I can help others similarly affected to overcome the problem and actually *enjoy* the journeys. Perhaps 'enjoy' is too bold a word, but we can drastically reduce the problem.

Basically, my mind and body suffered, initially, from a combination of the following:

1. Fear of the boat capsizing or taking in water (not good in the Arctic).
2. Discomfort in the stomach from the movement of the boat.
3. Eyes and stomach working independently thereby not forming a unifying sensation of the movement (producing bodily confusion).

4. Pitch, Roll, Yaw, Heave etc. all combined to produce a very complex motion.
5. One's own movements also compound with those of Problem 4.

Initially, I tried to overcome Problem 2 by positioning myself in the best orientation. This was found to be on my back laterally across the boat. The majority of beds are aligned that way anyhow! So the worst motion, the boat's roll, is turned through 90° and one's own body has a 'pitching' motion, which isn't as bad! That means that the feet go down and the head goes up and vice versa. The lesser problem of the boat's pitching is transformed into a slight rolling of one's own body from side to side, provided that one is truly lying flat on one's back and not partially or fully on one's side. I found that, unless one is truly flat that way, a confused feeling of complex motions was created.

In the flat position, if one also closes one's eyes, then the mind's confusion over conflicting sights and body movements (Problem 3) is eliminated, or at least substantially reduced. This also helps to reduce the effects of Problem 4.

Apart from the vessel's complex and irregular movements being misinterpreted by eyes, brain and stomach, further stomach/brain confusions seem to be compounded if one's own body is deliberately moved about (Problem 5). Thus, to move about one's cabin or even on the bed, will only aggravate an already complex situation into an unbearable one by going 'over the top' of one's personal limits.

To overcome this problem, my findings included the following:

(i) To save getting up for anti-sickness tablets, sweets,

breath-fresheners etc., put these on a bedside chair or table within reach of one's arm, and without having to move one's body. That is, they must be reachable ONLY by movements of the arm.

(ii) When even that is insufficient, put the required sweets or tablets in one's pockets, thereby allowing them to be located with even less movement, including ZERO movement of the eyes!

My trip helped me to conquer the psychosomatic problems (Problems 2–5) but only just, before reaching Bergen on the southwards leg.

I haven't mentioned the solution to Problem 1 yet, which I cured a bit earlier. I had experimented with:

(a) Looking out of the porthole to correlate eye and stomach effects whilst seeing that the boat's rolls and pitches were not too severe.

(b) NOT looking out of the porthole, both in calm and rough conditions.

(c) Instructing my mind about the statistics of boats capsizing and 'taking on water'.

Dealing with (c) first, since these Hurtigruten have been doing this route every day for 100 years (2,500 miles per day in total running time) without such problems, why should it happen now after 2,500 × 365 × 100 (i.e. over 91 million) miles? Thus I was convinced of the proven safety record of these boats! Problem solved!

Even when it *felt* rough, I initially tried Method (a) above, and it proved to be not as violent as it felt. Having satisfied myself on (a) and (c), I therefore adopted Method (b) for comfort, cosiness and the avoidance of Problem 5.

Those eleven days, of 2,500 miles, enabled me to 'cure' my lifelong problem of motion-sickness. This was partly Mind over Matter, partly Mind over Mind, but also Matter over Matter (i.e. the body).

Annex D
On the Bridge

On arrival on the Bridge, I was welcomed by two guys, both verbally and gastronomically. The gastronomic greeting was demonstrated by Norwegian coffee and waffles, which I consumed whilst chatting mainly with the crewman who did the steering and used the radars. It was my lucky day, the 13th, but the *previous* day had been Friday!

I had previously heard from my Dutch lady friends that there wasn't a 'big wheel' to steer with – just a very small one. This, indeed, proved to be the case. There was a *10cm radar* continuously surveilling the scene and plotting targets onto a display, normally with a 6-mile range with our own position offset to the bottom of the screen. The helmsman didn't usually employ the 'range rings', but when he did they were separated with half-mile spacings as their 'default'.

Judging by his answers, there was no MTI (Moving Target Indicator) facility and no PC (Pulse Compression) either. When attempting to demonstrate possible answers, his 'controls' only changed the 'gain control' with the inevitable loss of small targets! Whichever way the boat steered, and it weaved about a lot, the 'straight ahead' direction was always at the top of the screen.

'Boxes' of data could be created at the side of the main

map, and selected 'targets' would have their data displayed. He also selected 'clutter plots' to prove the answers were reasonable. Herein probably lies the reason why no MTI techniques were used on the radar – MTI is essential when most targets on the screen are aircraft. However, the most likely things to run into one's own boat there were not *moving* targets, but any one of the estimated 100,000 islands up the coast *en route*. Clearly, the navigator/pilot has to see all of these on his screen, or at least the nearest ones anyway! This is not the 'clutter' of the radar screens for controlling aircraft, but significant obstacles that one must *miss*. The rain clutter appeared as 'wispier' smudges on the display.

The boat was under manually-assisted autopilot almost the whole way. It was not programmed for the whole journey (Heaven forbid!) but manually set by twiddling a small knob between thumb and forefinger. Once twiddled, the boat continues on that heading no matter what the sea is doing. The heading is displayed in the digits alongside the speed digits which the autopilot also controls (normally set to approximately 15 knots).

To enable the digital heading-setting to have a 'meaning', that course is displayed on the screen, and the boat unerringly is threaded through the myriads of islands. The helmsman's course-setting activities, which involved a rapid twiddle to the desired heading, certainly explained the high roll-rates in turns that I'd noticed from the *discomfort* of my own cabin.

The helmsman only came off the automatic pilot's presettings when 'docking' or steering precisely along a narrow channel. This would be used in conditions where the submerged channel boundaries are not even visible to the passenger except by peering down into the water over the side of the boat when there was daylight. There were many such occasions during the long voyage.

I did not witness any noticeable processing with the Sonar system which they undoubtedly use. The submerged channels had to be navigated very carefully, sometimes by lights, sometimes by markers, sometimes by Sonar!

My query on radio-beacons wasn't understood (although he understood light-beacons) and it got the same response as my question on Satellite Navigation. On the latter, however, he did show me the GPS (Global Positioning System) equipment and its display. The display had push-button controls and a sort of 'windows technology' assistance in its computer dialogue.

My questions about identifying and distinguishing targets from clutter may not have been understood. A specific question, for example, 'How did you identify that target on the screen as a boat and not a small island?' produced the answer, accompanied by a pointing gesture to starboard, of 'I could see it over there!'

I followed that with questions about recognition in conditions of fog and darkness (i.e. distinguishing between clutter and targets) but I could not get any satisfactory answers. I felt sure that, had we both spoken the same language technically, matters might well have been improved – on the assumption that he was a technical man and not just a user of the equipment. Questions about EMC were not really understood, either, for the same reason, severe interference on the 10cm radar display prompting my questions on this.

Altogether it was an interesting diversion from previous sightseeing and it gave me different perspectives on 'motoring along the coast' and shipboard radars as opposed to airborne and ground-borne radars with which I had the expertise. I was very much indebted to my Norwegian friends for this technical demonstration.